The
Teaching
Portfolio

Capturing the
Scholarship in Teaching

by
Russell Edgerton
Patricia Hutchings
Kathleen Quinlan

A publication of
The AAHE Teaching Initiative
American Association for Higher Education

Routledge
Taylor & Francis Group

NEW YORK AND LONDON

We are deeply grateful to the Carnegie Corporation of New York for its support of this monograph.

THE TEACHING PORTFOLIO
Capturing the Scholarship in Teaching
by Russell Edgerton, Patricia Hutchings, and Kathleen Quinlan

© 1991 American Association for Higher Education, One Dupont Circle, Suite 360, Washington, DC 20036; ph 202/293-6440; www.aahe.org

First published in 1991 by Stylus Publishing, LLC.

Published in 2023 by Routledge
605 Third Avenue, New York, NY 10017
4 Park Square, Milton Park, Abingdon, Oxon OX14 4RN

Routledge is an imprint of the Taylor & Francis Group, an informa business.

ISBN: 9781563770036 (pbk)
ISBN: 9781003448136 (ebk)

DOI: 10.4324/9781003448136

Contents

Foreword

In 1987, several of us on the AAHE staff became involved in a family of major projects, inspired and funded by the Carnegie Corporation of New York, that addressed the need to improve America's schools and higher education's role in achieving that aim. The underlying theme of all these projects was that to improve the schools, teaching at all levels needed to be remade into a truly respected profession.

We found ourselves in the midst of a fascinating and (to us) new world of people, literature, and ideas about teaching. We were especially drawn to the work of Lee Shulman, professor of education and psychology at Stanford. Shulman's research demonstrated that effective teaching was much more subtle and complex than the conventional attention to "generic methods" assumed; that it had much to do with how well and deeply teachers understood the concepts they were teaching, and how these concepts could be communicated to ever-changing populations of students. Shulman's ideas, we learned, were providing the foundation for radically new approaches to the preparation and assessment of teachers.

It soon dawned on us that these ideas had enormous implications for how one might approach the improvement of teaching in higher education, as well. Rather than champion this or that mode or example of effective teaching, perhaps we should address the deeper question: Why don't university faculty see teaching as a subject worthy of intellectual discussion and study? Wouldn't teaching be improved if they did? What might be done to help that happen?

We tried these questions out on several hundred faculty who gathered at AAHE's National Conference on Higher Education to share their views about exemplary teaching. Heartened by their response, and funded with a gift from Allen Jossey-Bass, in April 1990 we launched the AAHE Teaching Initiative — a new program within

AAHE, under the direction of Patricia Hutchings. In June 1990, we announced our first major project: a three-year effort, funded by Lilly Endowment Inc., to develop "cases" of teaching episodes that could prompt deeper and richer conversations about teaching. Our second project is this monograph on the teaching portfolio; it aims, too, to provoke new conversations about teaching.

Many colleagues have contributed to this monograph. We initially turned to Peter Seldin, professor of management at Pace University, to scout the terrain and write an essay on the concept of the teaching portfolio. Seldin's reconnaissance turned up many valuable leads to work in progress — many of which have shaped our thinking. His monograph, *The Teaching Portfolio*, is available from Anker Publishing (see Resources).

During the past year, Pat Hutchings and I decided to explore further the distinctive potential of portfolios to capture the complexities of actual teaching. This potential, it seemed, was crucial to the larger purposes of AAHE's Teaching Initiative. We descended upon Lee Shulman and pawed through the files of his Stanford Teacher Assessment Project, a four-year effort to develop prototypes for assessing school teachers that could inform the work of the new National Board for Professional Teaching Standards. Many of the ideas about what portfolios might contain set forth in this monograph come from that visit. The materials developed by the members of the Stanford project team who served on the "biology task force" were especially helpful.

We are also much indebted to the cadre of Shulman's colleagues and graduate students who worked on the project and went on to publish articles about portfolios: Suzanne Wilson, Tom Bird, Angelo Collins, and Kenneth Wolf. Our discussion of the promise of portfolios in Chapter Two borrows heavily from Tom Bird's "An Essay on Possibilities." Our discussion of portfolio content in Chapter Three borrows heavily from Kenneth Wolf's article in *Phi Delta Kappan* magazine. This said, we haven't burdened the text with heavy footnoting.

Before directing the Teaching Initiative, Pat Hutchings served as director of AAHE's Assessment Forum. So she was aware that many campuses were turning to student portfolios as a way to assess the deeper understandings that students acquire over time. The campus experience with student portfolios represents still another source of ideas for us.

In the course of things, we also turned up a number of campuses that were already using or thinking of using portfolios or something like them. In the fall of 1990, we convened twenty-five "reflective practitioners" of portfolios for a day-long meeting, and have continued to rely on their wisdom. The campus practices we learned about through this group are highlighted here in the Appendix.

We used the occasion of AAHE's 1991 National Conference to ask four faculty members — Timothy Riordan, James Wilkinson, Judith Stanley, and Arthur Chickering — to work up samples of what a portfolio entry might look like. Their presentation, and the fact that several hundred people turned up for the session, was a great boost to our work. These entries (except for Judith Stanley's, which was on videotape) appear here in the Sample Entries section, along with others we've gathered since.

Last summer, Pat Hutchings and I vowed that we would get "something" about portfolios out the door. We were blessed with the arrival of Kathleen Quinlan, who appeared in the guise of a summer intern but in no time was operating as a colleague and cowriter. Kathleen did most of the roundup and editing of sample entries, then took part in the discussion and redrafting of each chapter.

What struck us as most useful at this stage was a monograph that set forth the case for using portfolios, advanced a point of view about the important issues of design, and offered a range of illustrations of what portfolio entries might look like. In the process of developing such a monograph, we were struck by the rightness of portfolios for evaluating *other* areas of faculty work as well — not only teaching but service and research. We toyed for a while with a title like "The Scholar's Portfolio," adding a tag that pointed to "the teaching dimension." We resisted that impulse, as you see, but the broader uses of the portfolio is a topic we return to in the final chapter, and one about which we have considerable hopes. In the meantime, we confine ourselves here to what seems a fruitful area for initial attention: teaching and its more authentic evaluation.

We would be the first to say that there is much work yet to be done in this area. Our hope is that this monograph will convince campuses that the *idea* of the teaching portfolio has sufficient potential that they should set about designing versions of their own.

Russell Edgerton
President, American Association for Higher Education
September 1991

Chapter 1

Teaching as a Scholarly Act

A movement that K. Patricia Cross labeled "Taking Teaching Seriously" is spreading throughout the country. Campus after campus is reexamining its commitment to teaching and beginning to explore ways that teaching might be rewarded and improved.

This movement is in part a response to important changes in public attitudes toward higher education. Students and parents, faced with the escalating costs of college attendance, are asking new and demanding questions about the value of undergraduate education. State policymakers are not only facing unrelenting budgetary demands; they are learning, through their involvement in the reform of schools, about "active learning" and other effective practices and wondering why colleges don't practice these too. In short, the heat is on.

But the new seriousness about teaching is also propelled from within academe. It is driven not only by presidents and trustees who want to reposition their campuses as teaching institutions but by faculty who care deeply about teaching and sense a new legitimacy for their concerns in the emerging interest in undergraduate reform.

For both external and internal reasons, then, we see this as an opportune moment to consider the role of teaching in higher education. But how will that opportunity unfold? How deep will this reexamination go? Will campuses simply make cosmetic changes and issue empty proclamations? Or will they reexamine such basic academic practices as the grounds for hiring and promoting faculty?

We believe that many campuses are indeed grappling with fundamental issues of practice, especially that lurking academic octopus, "the reward system." Moreover, there have now emerged some fresh perspectives from which these slippery old issues can be tackled. Two of these new perspectives are especially pertinent to the teaching portfolio.

The first new perspective is contained in *Scholarship Reconsidered*, a report issued in 1990 by the Carnegie Foundation for the Advancement of Teaching. In this report, Ernest Boyer argues that it is time to reformulate the tired debate about teaching *versus* research. Boyer argues that the categories of teaching, research, and service have become too segregated. Instead, we should begin with the premise that all faculty, whatever type of institution they might be working in, are *scholars*. Then we should consider the various ways in which their scholarship is expressed. Drawing on a formulation of scholarly roles developed by Eugene Rice (now provost at Antioch College), Boyer makes a case for thinking of faculty work in terms of four, overlapping functions: the scholarship of *discovery* (as in specialized research); the scholarship of *integration* (as in writing a textbook); the scholarship of *application* (as in consulting); and the scholarship of *teaching*.

This last category is, we think, particularly hard to grasp. What does it mean to talk about "the scholarship of teaching"? At bottom, the concept entails a view that teaching, like other scholarly activities (whether by Boyer's labels or by the more traditional ones of research, service, and teaching) relies on a base of expertise, a "scholarly knowing" that needs to and *can* be identified, made public, and evaluated; a scholarship that faculty themselves must be responsible for monitoring. That's a task, we'll argue in the pages that follow, that the teaching portfolio is distinctly suited to.

The second new perspective that bears on the teaching portfolio can be found in the stream of research authored and sponsored by Lee Shulman, professor of education and psychology at Stanford University. As we described in the Foreword, whereas the Carnegie report *asserts* that teaching is an expression of scholarship, Shulman's research explicates what the knowledge base of teaching actually is.

Shulman's research approach is itself novel. By and large, educators and psychologists who study teaching have concerned themselves with developing scientific principles about teaching — principles that would stand up to the tests of social science. But in doing so, Shulman believes, they have abstracted teaching from the particular situations — the fluid, untidy, unstructured realities of classroom life — in which teaching takes place. They have neglected the "knowing" in teaching that is hard to codify into scientific principles but is nonetheless a crucial part of teaching expertise.

Shulman illustrates this point through the analogy of chess playing. We recognize, he says, that a master chess player knows things that an ordinary chess player does not. But this knowledge is not a knowledge of principles; it is a knowledge of situations and ways of responding to them — the knowledge that comes of *having been there before*, and of *which precedents might best apply* in a new situation (in press).

Through intensive observation of practicing teachers, Shulman concluded that "master" teachers know many things that ordinary teachers do not. Most importantly, they have a command of the "pedagogy of substance" — a repertoire of ways to *transform* the particular concepts of their field into terms that can be under- stood by the particular students they teach. The exemplary economics teacher doesn't simply define "the demand curve" and gallop on to the next concept; rather, she knows a range of ways to help students understand the concept, apply it, and internalize it as their own.

Taken together, Boyer's call for broadening our view of scholarship and Shulman's vision of the knowing that informs good teaching form a conception of teaching as an act of scholarship. No longer can we think of teaching in the terms of the old formula: subject-matter expertise plus generic methods (how to plan a lecture, lead a discussion group . . .) equals good teaching. Effec- tive teaching is also a matter of transforming one's knowledge of a subject in ways that lead to student understanding.

This view of teaching will not, we're aware, surprise faculty who are experienced teachers; they know at a deep level the kinds of things that Shulman's research confirms. However, these insights are *not*, typically, the topic of conversa- tion in conferences and workshops about teach- ing; nor is a faculty member's ability to transform knowledge in ways that particular students can grasp at a deep level the basis for the evaluation of collegiate teaching. The teaching portfolio can, we believe, help document and display a concep- tion of teaching that is indeed a "pedagogy of sub- stance" — recognized and valued as a form of scholarly work.

Chapter 2

The Promise of Portfolios

What is a teaching portfolio? Why should anyone bother with it? What purposes can portfolios serve, and what distinctive advantages do they offer?

In an essay on the possibilities inherent in the concept of portfolios, Tom Bird observes that they would be much less appealing if they were called "the teacher's personnel file" (p. 242). Indeed, the suggestiveness of the notion lies in the analogy to portfolios kept by architects, designers, painters, and photographers to display their best work. What would happen, Bird asks, if teachers borrowed that practice? What would a "teaching portfolio" look like? How would it work?

The Power of Analogy

Beginning, as Bird does, with a view of the teaching portfolio as a suggestive analogy is precisely right, we think. It makes clear a point with which this monograph also begins: that there is no single thing called "a teaching portfolio"; neither the concept nor its practice is all figured out. What we have now are ideas (and also lots of questions) about what a teaching portfolio *might* be.

Within higher education, one such idea appears in a line of work begun in Canada some years ago under the aegis of the Canadian Association of University Teachers (CAUT). With an aim to improve the body of evidence about teaching that administrators could take into account in personnel actions, CAUT published a guide called *The Teaching Dossier* (Shore 1986). According to this guide, a teaching dossier is "a summary of a professor's major teaching accomplishments and strengths. It is to a professor's teaching what lists of publications, grants, and academic honors are to research" (p. 1). Peter Seldin's recent monograph, *The Teaching Portfolio,*

employs an almost identical definition, adding, "It is a factual description of a professor's major strengths and teaching achievements" (p. 3).

Here, then, is a first image of the teaching portfolio — the portfolio as a kind of "extended teaching resume." Indeed, Seldin recommends that faculty think of their portfolio as a "special insert" in their curriculum vitae under the heading of "Teaching" (p. 8). These portfolios aim for a brief but comprehensive account of teaching activity over a defined period of time.

Still other images of what portfolios might be appear in versions of them now being used on campuses across the country. Evergreen State College has long used portfolios as the primary tool for decisions about promotion and tenure; they consist primarily of self-reflective essays by faculty. At Roberts Wesleyan College, the emphasis is on faculty development; portfolios there are being incorporated into a "faculty growth contract" and are kept separate from personnel decision making. At the University of Pittsburgh, portfolios have recently been used in the selection of teaching-award winners; a wide range of materials are included, from annotated student work samples to self-reflective statements of teaching philosophy.

Yet another image of what a portfolio might be appears in the work of Stanford's Teacher Assessment Project. Kenneth Wolf, a member of the project team, drawing on earlier work by Tom Bird, describes possibilities that the group considered:

> *Should the school teacher's portfolio be more like a photographer's presentation of his very best work, or the pilot's log in which every flight is recorded? Should the portfolio display all of a person's work — the good, the bad, and the ugly — or only the work that the person is most proud of? Or, is teaching so dissim-*

ilar from any of these occupations that the model for the school teacher's portfolio should not be borrowed from any of these existing images? (p. 134)

Wolf and his colleagues came down on the side of the portfolio as a *display of best work*. In their view, the portfolio need not be a *comprehensive* record of performance over time, but a *selective* account — one that highlights what is unique about an individual's approach to teaching. Thus, the organizing image emerging from the Stanford project is of portfolios more like those used by professional artists, who provide samples of their best work to illustrate their distinctive style.

So what is a teaching portfolio? In the broadest sense, the teaching portfolio is a container into which many different ideas can be poured. Rather than settle on any fixed view of what the "it" is, we hope that campuses will explore many images of what portfolios might be.

At the same time, it seems to us that some versions of the portfolio are likely to be much more powerful in advancing good teaching — and therefore more learning — than others. Thus, this monograph describes and argues for a rather particular image of the portfolio.

At the heart of the portfolio as we envision it are *samples of teaching performance*: not just what teachers say about their practice but artifacts and examples of what they actually do. We argue, too, that portfolios should be *reflective*: work samples would be accompanied by faculty commentary and explanation that reveal not only what was done but why, the thinking behind the teaching. Finally, we argue for portfolios that are structured and selective: not (as one practitioner of portfolios for student assessment put it) "pack-ratting run rampant," but a careful selection of evidence organized around agreed upon categories, which themselves represent key dimensions of the scholarship of teaching.

What excites us about this image, and informs our view of what the portfolio might contain, is its potential for fostering the creation of a culture in which thoughtful discourse about teaching becomes the norm.

Why Bother? The Case for Portfolios

Since portfolios can take different shapes and serve various purposes, the case for developing them will vary as well. The strongest case, however — one that applies to a variety of types of portfolios but particularly to the one type described in our next chapter — can be captured in four interrelated propositions.

First, portfolios can capture the intellectual substance and "situated-ness" of teaching in ways that other methods of evaluation cannot. Second, because of this capacity, portfolios encourage faculty to take important, new roles in the documentation, observation, and review of teaching. Third, because they prompt faculty to take these new roles, portfolios are a particularly powerful tool for improvement. Fourth, as more faculty come to use them, portfolios can help forge a new campus culture of professionalism about teaching.

1. Portfolios capture the complexities of teaching.

A fillet knife can be used to chop up many things in the kitchen. But until we use it to fillet fish, we aren't exploiting the potential inherent in its particular design. So it is, we believe, with portfolios. Portfolios, as Shulman notes,

> . . . *are messy to construct, cumbersome to store, difficult to score, and vulnerable to misrepresentation. But in ways that no other assessment method can, portfolios provide a connection to the contexts and personal histories that characterize real teaching and make it possible to document the unfolding of both teaching and learning over time* (Shulman 1988).

Through portfolios, faculty can present evidence and reflection about their teaching in ways that keep this evidence and reflection *connected* to the particulars of what is being taught to whom under what conditions. As later sections of this monograph will make clear, in preparing entries for their portfolios, faculty can present concrete "pictures" of their practice: successive syllabi of a course that has evolved over time, "before and after" samples of student work, videotapes of lessons on key concepts, and so forth.

Moreover, in a portfolio, faculty can arrange and "annotate" these pictures in ways that document an overall approach to teaching. Entries constitute samples of larger performance; they function as cases in point. In this sense, portfolios constitute a considerable advance over the practice of classroom visits by an outside observer, a method of evaluation that at best provides only an isolated snapshot. With portfolios, discrete pictures of teaching can be presented in their context as part of an ongoing "documentary movie," a larger story. When maintained over several semesters, the portfolio can even allow a look at the gradual unfolding of expertise in a way that no other method makes possible.

2. **Portfolios place responsibility for evaluating teaching in the hands of faculty.**

Portfolios not only have properties that enable us to illuminate deeper dimensions of teaching; they enable faculty — indeed, *require* them — to become more important actors in monitoring and evaluating the quality of their own work.

First and most obviously, portfolios entail a shift of initiative. When it comes to research, faculty take it for granted that it is their responsibility to present evidence of accomplishment. In the case of teaching, however, evaluation often appears to be something that happens *to* faculty — be it through student course ratings or obligatory classroom visits by chairs or deans. Portfolios place the initiative for documenting and displaying teaching back in the hands of the person who is *doing* it; they put the teacher back in charge . . . selecting, assembling, and explaining portfolio entries that accurately represent actual performance.

Second, portfolios invite faculty to participate in the examination of *one another's* teaching. Faculty can work collaboratively in constructing their portfolios; they can also use portfolios as windows to view and share perspectives on one another's teaching. Such collaboration is almost certain to be powerful where the aim is to improve teaching. When teaching is being evaluated for purposes of personnel decisions, faculty collaboration around portfolios might constitute a real sea change.

The contrast with prevailing practice is striking. On most campuses, student ratings are the "method of choice" for evaluating teaching, supplemented by a classroom visit or two and perhaps testimonial letters. By and large, faculty colleagues are not involved, or only secondarily as judges of evidence and perspectives submitted by others. What is "peer reviewed" is not the process of teaching and its products (the learning that the teaching enabled) but the observations and ratings submitted by students and assorted others.

This situation is in part a function of faculty uneasiness about the intrusion of colleagues in their classrooms. But underneath this unease lies a more troubling circumstance: the lack of clarity about why faculty *should* be observers of one another's teaching.

This lack of clarity is no surprise. One need only note that the aspects of teaching most often evaluated are classroom management and interpersonal skills. We ask how clear the assignments are, whether grades are fair, how promptly student work is returned, whether student ideas are respected . . . questions students are indeed qualified to answer.

But there's more to teaching than what's critiqued on student evaluation forms. What's missing in such evaluation are precisely those aspects of teaching that *faculty* are uniquely qualified to observe and judge: issues about how appropriately courses are organized, whether crucial content is covered (and more incidental material left out), and how well key concepts are represented. In short, there are aspects of the teaching/learning transaction — those things Lee Shulman has in mind when he refers to "the pedagogy of substance" — that *require* peer perspectives and review.

Here is where portfolios can help. Classroom visitation is a desirable practice; it's a form of peer review that can indeed address the most substantive, scholarly aspects of teaching. But classroom visitation is far from universal. Many campuses practice it not at all; some do so in only perfunctory ways. The good news is that portfolios offer an attractive, nonthreatening *step toward* classroom visitation. A professor can work up samples of her teaching, including videotapes, and present them to her colleagues for comment; her colleagues can observe her teaching without setting foot in her classroom. In time, we hope, as faculty come to appreciate through work on portfolios the value of peer perspectives, classroom visitation will seem a natural next step.

Finally, portfolios involve faculty in setting *standards* for effective teaching. An entry in "Professor Smith's" portfolio includes a creative assignment in a biology lab. Do his colleagues in the department agree with Smith that this is a creative and appropriate way to teach the principles of genetics involved in this assignment? Do they believe that the teaching in question will lead to *learning?* What kinds of learning — what levels of understanding — do they believe most matter in the teaching of genetics? These are some of the questions that the review of the portfolio might naturally raise; the "answers" (obviously such questions won't have any single answer) constitute an important step toward the articulation of standards for effective teaching. And with a *set* of portfolios on the table for review and discussion, larger, collective discussion of campus expectations for teaching can occur.

3. Portfolios can prompt more reflective practice and improvement.

There are many routes to the improvement of teaching, but teaching portfolios can have a special power to involve faculty in reflection on their own practice and how to improve it. This potential for improvement is the single most-cited benefit of portfolio use to date.

The reasons are not hard to understand. In the very process of assembling portfolios, faculty reflect on their teaching: selecting best work, organizing evidence so that it creates a larger, authentic picture of their practice. Because faculty are the makers of their own portfolios, the level of "investment" is also high — a necessary condition for change, and one that is sometimes missing in evaluation by student rating.

Moreover, because portfolios display not only the final products of teaching but its processes — the thoughts behind the actions — they also

reveal much about teaching to colleagues involved in the development and review of portfolios. Whether at the department level or across departments, occasions where faculty examine one another's portfolios could be occasions for cultivating new and richer ways of thinking about and inquiring into the scholarship of teaching, which brings us to the portfolio's fourth advantage.

4. Portfolios can foster a culture of teaching and a new discourse about it.

Teaching is examined at many points and occasions in a faculty member's life. On the one hand, there are all the occasions at which personnel decisions are made: hiring, assigning course workloads, annual evaluations for salary and promotion, the granting or withholding of tenure. And on the other hand, there are occasions and processes where the agenda is not to judge or select but to diagnose and improve: consultation with instructional-development professionals, mentoring programs, and team teaching, for example.

Teaching portfolios can introduce more compelling, authentic evidence about teaching into all of these occasions. Annual-review and tenure committees might require candidates to submit portfolios as evidence of their teaching performance. But institutions or departments might also turn to portfolios purely to cultivate a more thoughtful discussion about the elements of good teaching.

Are some uses for portfolios better — or more appropriate — than others? The underlying theme of this monograph is that there is a scholarship in teaching that has yet to be fully acknowledged and discussed; bringing that scholarship out in the open would enrich faculty discourse about teaching and cultivate a new respect for the profession of teaching. In truth, the teaching portfolio is a technology yet to be invented for a culture that on many campuses doesn't yet exist — a culture of professional inquiry about good teaching. We believe that the kind of portfolio described in the next chapter can help foster such a culture by uncovering the scholarship in teaching.

Chapter 3

The Format and Content of a Portfolio

What should go into a portfolio? What would a "typical" portfolio look like? Obviously, the different understandings about what portfolios are, and the different ways they can be used, all have bearing on the determination of what a portfolio should contain. The first step in sorting through the possibilities, in our view, is to be clear about the *reasons* why a campus might wish to prescribe the format or content of a portfolio in the first place.

Determining Needs and Purposes

Portfolios, as we've said, can be used for purposes ranging from evaluating a candidate for promotion and tenure to facilitating good conversation about teaching; *which* use one intends will drive decisions about format and content. The more the portfolio becomes a basis for important personnel decisions, for example, the more likely it is that people will feel the need for *requiring* that it contain specified (even uniform) kinds of information.

Consider the "possible items for inclusion" listed in the 1986 Canadian Association of University Teachers publication *The Teaching Dossier* (Shore), shown on page 8. The forty-nine items are grouped under the headings "The Products of Good Teaching," "Material From Oneself," and "Information From Others." For purposes or occasions of professional development, it's possible to imagine a portfolio that includes *no* "information from others" — such as student ratings and colleague evaluations. But in making decisions about promotion and tenure, most committees charged with this task would want to see *many* kinds of evidence — including ratings from students and evaluations from colleagues.

Another circumstance that might affect portfolio contents is that in which portfolios are being compared with one another. For example, port-folios might be used (and are on several campuses) for selecting candidates to receive a teaching award. The need here is for some degree of standardization, some common structure that enables reviewers to compare portfolios.

The experience of campuses with *student* portfolios offers an instructive lesson on this point. The College of William and Mary, looking for an alternative to standardized tests, turned to portfolios to examine student learning in general education. They started with open-ended portfolios and quickly discovered that without common categories of evidence, the portfolios were impossible to evaluate. The College is now working to design more structured portfolios for assessing student learning and program effects.

Both CAUT's *Teaching Dossier* and Seldin's *The Teaching Portfolio* — the only two general guidelines now available — recognize these considerations of purpose and how they affect the issue of portfolio contents. But it is noteworthy that neither takes a position on the relative value of the options. CAUT offers the forty-nine "possible items for inclusion" to stimulate faculty thinking on what choices they might consider, but there is no framework provided for choosing among them.

The Portrayal of Teaching

There is, however, *another* perspective from which one might derive ideas about portfolio format and content: that is, a perspective about *how teaching can best be documented and displayed*, which, in turn, presumes a view of *teaching itself*. That is, the more we understand about what is important in teaching, the more we understand about how acts of teaching can best be captured and revealed for others to review. It is from those understandings that one comes to a recognition of the importance of a framework for determining

Possible items for inclusion

Faculty members should recognize which of the items which might be included in a teaching dossier would most effectively give a favorable impression of teaching competence and which might better be used for self-evaluation and improvement. The dossier should be compiled to make the best possible case for teaching effectiveness.

THE PRODUCTS OF GOOD TEACHING

1. Students' scores on teacher-made or standardized tests, possibly before and after a course has been taken as evidence of learning.
2. Student laboratory workbooks and other kinds of workbooks or logs.
3. Student essays, creative work, and project or field-work reports.
4. Publications by students on course-related work.
5. A record of students who select and succeed in advanced courses of study in the field.
6. A record of students who elect another course with the same professor.
7. Evidence of effective supervision of Honors, Master's or Ph.D. theses.
8. Setting up or running a successful internship program.
9. Documentary evidence of the effect of courses on student career choice.
10. Documentary evidence of help given by the professor to students in securing employment.
11. Evidence of help given to colleagues on teaching improvement.

MATERIAL FROM ONESELF

Descriptive material on current and recent teaching responsibilities and practices.

12. List of course titles and numbers, unit values or credits, enrolments with brief elaboration.
13. List of course materials prepared for students.
14. Information on professor's availability to students.
15. Report on identification of student difficulties and encouragement of student participation in courses or programs.
16. Description of how films, computers or other nonprint materials were used in teaching.
17. Steps taken to emphasize the interrelatedness and relevance of different kinds of learning.

Description of steps taken to evaluate and improve one's teaching.

18. Maintaining a record of the changes resulting from self-evaluation.
19. Reading journals on improving teaching and attempting to implement acquired ideas.
20. Reviewing new teaching materials for possible application.
21. Exchanging course materials with a colleague from another institution.
22. Conducting research on one's own teaching or course.
23. Becoming involved in an association or society concerned with the improvement of teaching and learning.

24. Attempting instructional innovations and evaluating their effectiveness.
25. Using general support services such as the Education Resources Information Centre (ERIC) in improving one's teaching.
26. Participating in seminars, workshops and professional meetings intended to improve teaching.
27. Participating in course or curriculum development.
28. Pursuing a line of research that contributes directly to teaching.
29. Preparing a textbook or other instructional materials.
30. Editing or contributing to a professional journal on teaching one's subject.

INFORMATION FROM OTHERS

Students:

31. Student course and teaching evaluation data which suggest improvements or produce an overall rating of effectiveness or satisfaction.
32. Written comments from a student committee to evaluate courses and provide feedback.
33. Unstructured (and possibly unsolicited) written evaluations by students, including written comments on exams and letters received after a course has been completed.
34. Documented reports of satisfaction with out-of-class contacts.
35. Interview data collected from students after completion of a course.
36. Honors received from students, such as being elected "teacher of the year".

Colleagues:

37. Statements from colleagues who have observed teaching either as members of a teaching team or as independent observers of a particular course, or who teach other sections of the same course.
38. Written comments from those who teach courses for which a particular course is a prerequisite.
39. Evaluation of contributions to course development and improvement.
40. Statements from colleagues from other institutions on such matters as how well students have been prepared for graduate studies.
41. Honors or recognition such as a distinguished teacher award or election to a committee on teaching.
42. Requests for advice or acknowledgement of advice received by a committee on teaching or similar body.

Other sources:

43. Statements about teaching achievements from administrators at one's own institution or from other institutions.
44. Alumni ratings or other graduate feedback.
45. Comments from parents of students.
46. Reports from employers of students (e.g., in a work-study or "cooperative" program).
47. Invitations to teach for outside agencies.
48. Invitations to contribute to the teaching literature.
49. Other kinds of invitations based on one's reputation as a teacher (for example, a media interview on a successful teaching innovation).

what goes into a teaching portfolio.

Here, we believe, is where the Stanford Teacher Assessment Project has a major contribution to make to portfolio design. In the course of the project, the team came up with a number of provocative ideas about what kind of portfolio "entries" would be most revealing about a teacher's approach to teaching. And they also developed some ideas about how these entries could be arrayed so as to present a reasonably complete picture of that teacher's performance.

Reflecting on Samples of Actual Performance

The Stanford team began with the premise that portfolios should be based in actual performance. The team was unwilling to allow teachers (as some campus versions of portfolios now do) simply to report what they did in their classroom. Reflective essays *alone* would not do. "The aim," as Kenneth Wolf put it, is to look at "what teachers actually do, not what they *say* they do" (p. 132).

In addition to believing that portfolios should be connected to actual performance, the project team worked on the premise that good teaching was highly situational. Teachers were not simply good "in general." Whether they were good or not depended on the *particulars* of the situation — exactly what was being taught to whom and under what conditions. So to capture good teaching, the team decided that it was important to zero in on *particular episodes* of actual teaching. They assumed, in short, that the more complex aspects of good teaching would best be revealed by looking at *discrete samples of actual work*.

What, then, might a work sample be? Well, the team decided, there were all the materials that are generated in the giving of a course: syllabi, daily assignments, special reading lists, laboratory exercises, student papers, student examinations . . . all the *artifacts* of teaching. And second, there were *reproductions* and representations of what happened: videotapes of classroom situations, photographs, diaries, journals. Both categories would provide evidence of what actually happened.

But, the team realized, these samples of actual work don't speak for themselves. To fill a portfolio with artifacts such as a syllabus, lesson plans, and student examinations would be like handing your secretary your "in-box" and saying, "Please act on these items right away." What's missing — what's *needed* — is an explanation.

And so we come to the punch line, the major insight we find in the work of the Stanford project. General reflection, divorced from evidence of actual performance, fails to capture the situated nature of teaching. Work samples alone aren't intelligible. But work samples *plus* reflection make a powerful formula. The reflection is "grounded" by being connected to a particular instance of teaching; the work sample is made meaningful and placed in context through reflection. Thus, out of the Stanford project comes a sense of what the character of a portfolio entry might be: a professor's reflections about a sample of actual work.

Covering the Critical Tasks of Teaching

We came away from our immersion in the Stanford project with the notion that reflections on samples of actual teaching can be the basic building blocks of a portfolio. But there remained another problem to be solved. Faculty preparing a portfolio of such entries, left to their own devices, might simply select samples from one small corner of their classroom work. Suppose a biologist prepared a portfolio that included only entries from the laboratory sections of the course. Anyone reviewing the portfolio would immediately ask, what of the rest of the experience? What, for instance, of this professor's ability to lecture or to help students make sense of textbook readings?

So, in addition to specifying the nature of portfolio entries, we need to confront the question: What should the sample entries be samples *of*? What guidance might any instructions for portfolio development provide about the domains of teaching performance that entries should reflect?

In our view, this is still an unsettled question. The answers might well vary according to the type of institution and discipline that the professor preparing the portfolio is in. Some campuses consider advising and out-of-classroom contact with students to be an important aspect of teaching performance. Others might feel that those activities have no place in the professorial role and therefore in a teaching portfolio. Similarly, to require an entry that focuses on teaching aimed at "experiential learning" might make sense in some disciplines but would need to be understood quite differently in English and nursing. There is much to be learned from experimenting with portfolios in diverse settings.

But there is an appealing place to start. In considering the issue of domain, the task force on the Stanford project that developed portfolios in the field of biology decided that every teacher confronted *four core tasks*:

- course planning and preparation;
- actual teaching;
- evaluating student learning and providing feedback; and
- keeping up with the professional field in areas related to teaching performance.

While not necessarily the final answer, we are taken with the simplicity of this scheme.

Examples of Entries for Each Task

Imagine, for example, that you are preparing a portfolio. You are required to prepare an entry that illustrates your approach to each of these four tasks. What might you include?

In the category of *course planning*, you might begin with the syllabus — or several syllabi — for a course revised over successive years. The syllabi would be your "work sample." The "reflective" portion of the entry might then be a commentary on why the current syllabus contains what it does, how it had changed from one year to the next and why. Had new literature appeared? Had your students changed? Had your experience of teaching the course given you new ideas about what did and did not work?

The syllabus, to be sure, is only one way to document course planning. Alternatively, the work sample might be a series of assignments that you gave your students throughout the semester. The reflective portion of the entry would be your rationale for each of the assignments as well as for the set as a whole. Or suppose you wished to

focus on the way you approached the teaching of a key concept in your field. Here, you might use your assignments and your lecture notes as your work sample. Your reflections might deal with how and why your approach to the concept has changed over time, with attention to the returns in student understanding.

For the second task — your actual *teaching of the course* — there are numerous possibilities. You might have a colleague visit your class and then base your reflections on the notes and observations your colleague produced. (There is much to be said for classroom visitation, but also — and particularly on campuses where faculty have little experience observing one another — some things to overcome: your colleague might not be a skilled observer, your students might behave differently in your colleague's presence, and so on.) Alternatively, you could develop an entry by having your teaching videotaped, then selecting segments that best reveal your distinctive style of teaching, accompanied by your reflection on those segments. Still another alternative would be to enlist several students in an effort to keep detailed journals, using these as the basis for your reflections.

The third task — *evaluating and giving feedback to students* about their work — also lends itself to many possibilities. You might take a student paper that illustrated a high standard of performance and comment on why the standard was appropriate, and what you had done as a teacher to enable the student to achieve that standard. Alternatively, you might use a paper or an exam that reflects misconceptions students often bring to the course, and then comment on how you handle those misconceptions. Such an entry would capture for public discussion a dimension of learning that educators have come to see as particularly key in the last decade.

An entire repertoire of ways to assess student learning and give feedback are available in the publications by K. Patricia Cross and Tom Angelo on "Classroom Research." The "one-minute paper" — a simple strategy designed to reveal what students did *and* didn't understand from a given class session — would be excellent grist for an entry that reflects on the gaps between what you as a teacher say on the one hand, and what students hear and learn on the other.

The fourth task — *keeping up with and contributing to one's field* — is clearly an important part of "staying alive" as a teacher. Most telling and useful would be entries that not only relate a professional experience but indicate its effect on teaching. Your work sample, for instance, might be a paper you heard at a professional meeting. Your reflective essay might then comment on how you used this new knowledge to change your approach to a course.

Wrap-up: Format of a Teaching Portfolio

Having now looked at the character of individual entries, one comes to questions about the whole. What might a complete portfolio look like? What format might it take? Again, there's no single answer; each campus needs to think through and design its own version of the portfolio. But here's a rough sketch of one possible version:

Section one might be called *Background Information*. Everyone reviewing a portfolio, no matter what kind of portfolio it is or how it will be used, will need a context for understanding the entries. Two categories of contextual information seem important.

The first is the professional biography of the person who is preparing the portfolio. At a minimum, this could be a traditional resume. But it might also be useful to have the person write about key stages in his or her development as a teacher.

The second is information about the specific environment in which the individual works . . . what the campus and department expect in terms of teaching, research, and service; what specific classes the individual faculty member teaches; and the important details about these classes that affect teaching — such as course size and the characteristics, abilities, and motivations of the students.

Section two might be called *Selected Entries*. If the teaching terrain were divided into the four critical tasks described above, then each of these tasks would become a subsection. Alternatively, portfolio guidelines might simply require the individual preparing the portfolio to document and

display entries that illustrated *diverse* aspects of his or her performance. Each entry would have a caption, and the various documents — be they artifacts, reproductions, or reflective commentary — would be clearly labeled.

How many entries is enough? The Stanford project — as we discuss further in Chapter Four — found that raters of portfolios made up their minds after reviewing just a few entries per category. More was not necessarily better. This is, to us, good news indeed; it reinforces our view that a selected, limited number of sample entries can be highly revealing.

For some purposes and occasions, portfolios with these two sections would suffice. For other purposes, a campus might wish to add *other sections of required information*.

Many campuses, when a critical personnel decision has to be made, for example, will want faculty to provide evaluations and ratings done by students, faculty peers, and/or administrators. Since such data can easily become unwieldy, careful thought should be given (as ever) to what data are really needed. Requiring all student rating sheets, for example, without any summary or perspective from which to view them, doesn't strike us as very sensible. On the other hand, a summary of the data, and — better yet — a reflective essay on how the professor responded to them, might be quite revealing.

Some campuses might ask faculty members to write reflective essays about their teaching that are not necessarily tied to particular acts of performance. A number of institutions, such as the University of Maryland's University College and Evergreen State College, do this now.

The list could go on. And of course the portfolio need not (and probably should not) be the only source of evidence for decisions about faculty; one might, for instance, decide that student evaluations provide important information but that they do not belong in the portfolio itself. The important point here — the image we most want to stress — is the portfolio as a set of entries that combine real work samples with reflection. That image leaves lots of maneuvering room, but within it we'd vote to keep portfolios as lean and lively as they can possibly be.

11

Sample Entries

It's one thing to talk about teaching portfolios in general, another to look at the particulars that might comprise one. To do so, we asked eight faculty from a variety of campus settings and disciplines to develop sample entries — entries based on the work-sample-plus-reflection model set forth in Chapter Three. We offer their entries here as a means of exploring more concretely the character of useful portfolio entries; as such, they seem to us to raise a number of interesting issues.

1. A first and fundamental issue is about **how to characterize** the entries here: What are they evidence *of*? Following the work of the Stanford project team, we argued earlier that a useful image for portfolios is as a selective display of "best work." But "best work" might not be the best label for what one observes in the entries set forth here. This is not to say that they don't *portray* exemplary practices; it *is* to say that their exemplariness is not what most strikes the reader.

It seemed to us, rather, that what one sees in most of the eight entries is evidence of reflectiveness: an ability (and willingness) to look one's performance in the eye, to step back from it, to assess strengths and weaknesses, to raise hard questions, and — importantly — to see routes to improvement. Donald Schön's work on "reflective practice" might be an appropriate framework for understanding the potential of portfolios.

Relatedly, in entries such as Tim Riordan's and Bill Whipple's — both of which examine the evolution of a course over time — we're struck by evidence of change and development. The capacity to document growth over time is, of course, one of the ways that portfolios improve on other methods of documentation. Nevertheless, we're left asking, what would a "best work" entry really look like? Is it something the field should be working toward?

2. A number of the entries rather immediately raise issues about **length**: How much of a sample do we need to see to get a sense of the larger weave? It should be said here that most of the entries that follow have been *abridged* and slightly *edited* for publication. We did so in order to keep the length of this monograph under control — but also because it seemed to us that less was sometimes sufficiently revealing. But we're aware, too, having shared several of these entries with faculty groups, that some readers will want more. In the case of James Wilkinson's entry — reflections on the evaluation of a student essay — some reviewers have responded, "We need to see *several* essays by this student in order to evaluate the rightness of Wilkinson's reflection."

There's unlikely to be any simple formula for "how much is enough," but further experimentation might get us closer to a sense of what is sufficient.

3. Related to the general issue of "how much" is a more particular one about the *relative* **usefulness** of the two aspects of the entry: work sample and reflection. One reader of the eight entries observed that the reflections carried most of the weight; for him, the work samples added little. Other readers — such as those responding to the Wilkinson entry with calls for further student papers — found themselves wanting more work samples. In theory, of course, the work sample "grounds" the reflection and gives it credibility, while the reflection gives meaning to work samples whose significance would otherwise be ambiguous. But that theory needs testing in practice.

4. Another set of issues arises around the model of the **four core tasks** of teaching proposed in Chapter Three. Our point in proposing them was not (as we say) that they're the only possible framework for entries, but that *some* structure

is needed and the four seem a useful place to begin. Nevertheless, our experience with the eight entries here (most of which were produced with one of the four tasks in mind) suggests that trying to match entries to *any* set of prescribed categories might be tricky business. For instance, an entry such as Jennifer Hicks's, based on Classroom Research she conducted in a composition course, might fit under either "evaluating student learning" or "keeping up with the field." The point is a simple but important one: that the boundaries between categories are ambiguous and overlapping. Their purpose is not to pigeon-hole or restrict but to provide an organizing structure for selecting, presenting, and interpreting material.

5. An obvious issue raised by the entries that follow is one of **representativeness.** No single entry — no matter how carefully and thoughtfully prepared — can (or should) be the sole basis for judgments about overall teaching performance. As argued earlier, one needs to see a range of entries representing a variety of teaching tasks. Exactly how many entries are needed, representing what span of time and activities, will depend on purpose and perhaps on other variables we need to know more about.

6. Finally, it might be useful to say something about **what the entries presented here are *not*.** They are not final, polished pieces of work; they are not "models" meant to be imitated. Rather, they are excerpts from first efforts, rough drafts, if you will, of a thing that is very much being invented. We look forward to discussion of these entries and the generation of others that will expand the repertoire.

* * * * * *

Many thanks to the faculty who volunteered these entries. Most of them prepared the samples at our request during what would otherwise have been summer vacation; many of them took on the task without knowing how long it would take; several willingly completed substantial revision. We appreciate not only the time and energy put forth by these busy people but the candor and risk taking that their entries represent. Their work confirms, we think, the power of the teaching portfolio to make teaching a more intellectually engaging, public enterprise.

* * * * * *

Contents

Rethinking Introductory Philosophy

This entry was volunteered by Timothy Riordan, professor of philosophy at Alverno College. The entry focuses on planning for Philosophy 210, an introductory-level course required for the major but also taken by students completing general-education requirements. Looking at two versions of the syllabus for this course, the first from 1986, the second from 1990, Dr. Riordan reflects on his changing conception of the course as reflected in differences between the two syllabi.

From 1986

Alverno College
3401 South 39th Street / Milwaukee, WI 53215

INSTRUCTIONAL SYLLABUS

TITLE: _Search for Meaning_

COURSE NUMBER: _Pl 210_   SECTION: _____

INSTRUCTOR: _Tim Riordan_

DEPT/DIV: _Philosophy/Arts and Humanities_

In this course students will read works by philosophers and other thinkers who suggest varying attitudes about the meaning and purpose of human existence. The emphasis in the course will be on classroom discussion so that students can grapple with the ideas of others in an attempt to develop their own views about basic human questions. Although the course will include works from philosophers throughout history, students will be expected to apply their ideas to life in the contemporary context.

1986

The Apology -- Plato

Man's Search for Meaning -- Viktor Frankl

The Stranger -- Albert Camus

On the Subjection of Women -- John Stuart Mill

The Virtue of Selfishness -- Ayn Rand

I Know Why the Caged Bird Sings -- Maya Angelou

Nectar in a Sieve -- Kamala Markandaya

I have been teaching an introductory philosophy course, "Search for Meaning," for several years now and have made some significant changes based on my experiences in the classroom, concern for meeting the particular needs of the students I teach, and an awareness of what has been happening in my discipline and in the contemporary world in general. One of the obvious shifts you can see is in the Introduction to the syllabus. I started out with a pretty general description of the issues and methods of the course, stressing the discussion of meaning in our lives. After I taught the course a couple of times, I decided that a central issue in many of our discussions was how to make commitments in a pluralistic and rapidly changing world. The revised Introduction reflects that emphasis and provides a much clearer and, I think, more meaningful framework for the students as they begin to consider what we will be about in the course. It takes them from the vague and abstract notion of "meaning" to the context in which they are trying to construct meaning in their own lives.

I have also changed required texts several times while teaching the course, and the most significant change is a little embarrassing to admit. Although I teach at a liberal arts college for women, the first couple of times I taught the course all of the required texts were written by men. I suppose this wasn't too surprising, since it reflected my own education, but I realized that I needed to find some works that connected more directly to my students' experience and that allowed voices into the classroom dis-

```
                                 Alverno College
                                 3401 South 39th Street / Milwaukee, WI 53215

INSTRUCTIONAL      SYLLABUS

TITLE:              SEARCH FOR MEANING

COURSE NUMBER:  PL 210                              SECTION:  All

INSTRUCTOR:       TIM RIORDAN

DEPT/DIV:         PHILOSOPHY/ARTS AND HUMANITIES
```

In the future when historians discuss the 20th Century, they will
probably stress the ever-increasing rate of change that is so
characteristic of our age. The discoveries of science and the
virtually world-wide dissemination of information via the mass media
have changed our lives in countless ways. Television has broadened
our horizon not only to distant states within our own country, but to
continents and cultures across the seas as well. Accomplishments
which used to make for great science fiction are taken for granted as
realities and people have begun to sense that just about anything is
possible. Absolute values and dogmatic statements are necessarily
viewed with scepticism, since there is an awareness that new
information might dissolve the authenticity of any absolute. As
people begin to gain knowledge of other cultures, they realize the
relative nature of their own culture's values. As they are exposed to
realities which shatter myths, they begin to wonder if anything is
sacred.

It is exciting to live at such a time in human history, but for many
it is also unbearably insecure. Those who have lived with a faith in
secure absolutes are finding rapid change and relativism difficult to
cope with. People associated with formal religion can no longer find
a simple description of what it means to be a good Catholic or
Protestant or Jew. Citizens are faced with new ideas of what
constitutes patriotism. Pluralism is simply a matter of fact in such
a changing world, and it is often a struggle to cope with that kind of
instability.

In this course we will focus on the contemporary search for meaning.
We will not propose simple answers to complex questions, but we will
examine the questions carefully and discuss suggested ways of
answering them. We will read works by philosophers and other
humanistic authors who provide varying attitudes toward basic
questions about human existence, and we will discuss their ideas with
an eye to developing our own outlook on a pluralistic world. The
point of the course is neither to confuse nor to comfort, but to
grapple honestly with the desire for certainty in an age of
uncertainty.
  0889
                                              WEEKDAY COLLEGE

1990

The Apology -- Plato

What Does It All Mean -- Thomas Nagel

My Brilliant Career (film)

On the Subjection of Women -- John Stuart Mill

The Virtue of Selfishness -- Ayn Rand

Duties to Oneself: An Ethical Basis for Self-Liberation -- Joan Starumanis

The Color Purple -- Alice Walker

The Plague -- Albert Camus
```

been especially concerned to find pieces that address the issue many of my students face: how to pursue one's own interest while remaining connected to others'. Many of the women I teach are raising families while going to school and are struggling with the responsibilities they feel for others and the sense emerging for them that they have rights themselves. I have used excerpts from Ayn Rand's *The Virtue of Selfishness* to address the issue, but have found that she doesn't deal with some of the complexity of the issue; so I now also use an article by Joan Starumanis, which provides more analysis of the problem and suggestions for dealing with it. Some other changes you will see in the required course materials reflect my growing concern for including different cultural perspectives as well.

course that were too often silenced. To this end, I started using material written by and about women and representatives of different cultures. I still use Plato's *Apology*, but I also use a film called *My Bril-liant Career*, which tells the story of a woman who challenges the culture of her time — a motif we look at in Socrates — but in a way and context that reflect the struggles of my own students. I have
```

How Students Learn in a Management Class

Richard N. Ottaway, professor of management at Fairleigh Dickinson University, prepared this entry describing a course on the fundamentals of management he taught in the fall of 1990. He includes the syllabus as his work sample; his reflections — excerpted here — focus on the pedagogical theory undergirding that syllabus and on how a changing mix of students will affect next versions of the course.

In the past, the great majority of my students in "Fundamentals of Management" have been part-time, working adults, and the design of the course has been largely driven by my view of adult learning. I employ a four-point cycle: Students are presented with a new theory or skill; they test or apply that theory or skill at work; they report back findings in a "teach-each-other" format; and they write an analytical critique of what they have learned. (See Ottaway, "Improving Learning for Adult Part-Time Students," in *The Department Chairperson's Role in Enhancing College Teaching*, Jossey-Bass, 1989.) Assignments are organized around this cycle; several assignments are also intended to make students more *aware* of this learning process — the analysis of the journal (assignment 3) for instance. I am convinced that part-time, adult students have a better learning experience when the pedagogy is designed to utilize their work or life experiences in the learning process. My pedagogy was tested against traditional lecture teaching and found to attain "a significantly higher merging of classroom materials with workplace realities and an increased awareness of the complexities of organizational

life" than those taught by traditional methods (see W.B. Fox, "Utility of an Andragogical Approach to Management Education: An Empirical Investigation," *The Organizational Behavior Teaching Review*, Vol. 14, no. 1, pp. 97-114).

However, the student composition of this course in Fall 1990 was different than my previous experience; there were many more full-time undergraduates than the course was designed to accommodate. What can be done to help the full-time students have an application experience like the part-time ones? In the past I would spread the few full-time

students around the "report-back" discussion groups and make them research assistants, scanning the major business periodicals for material to supplement the discussions. This works well for some students, but with the shift in class demographics, discussions tended to become less stimulating, students became disconnected from the course, and interest dropped. Consequently, when I teach the same course next time I am going to make three changes in it. The major difference will be that full-time students will bring a one-page response to the questions about a case that appear at the end

---

FAIRLEIGH DICKINSON UNIVERSITY
College of Business Administration

Fundamentals of Management   Dr. R.N. Ottaway
MG 201   221-1314 home
Fall 1990   593-8858 - office

<u>Course Outline</u>

The course will cover the fundamental concepts of management of a modern work organization, the characteristics of those persons involved in it, and a special focus on work in a global setting. The course will consist of lectures, discussions, readings, written work and examinations on the topics outlined below.

<u>Assignments</u>

One of the purposes of this course is to assist the student in developing the application of classroom material to the work place. In order to acomplish this, the following learning experiences are planned:

1. Keep a journal of observations of applications of classroom material in the work place. Guidelines for observations for each week are on page 3. Get a notebook for journal entries. Bring observations to class each week for discussion. Grade included in item 3.

2. Compose a 2 page paper stating why you are preparing yourself to work in a business organization, or if not, why not. Due on Session 2 and accounts for <u>10% of final grade</u>.

3. Summit a 2,500 word essay of the analysis of the journal comparing observations in the work place to theory. Due on session 14 and accounts for <u>15% of final grade</u>.

4. Exam I is an examination of sessions 1-5 on session 6 which accounts for <u>25% of final grade</u>.

5. Exam II is an examination of sessions 6-9a on session 11 which accounts for <u>25% of final grade</u>.

6. Exam III is an examination of sessions 9b-14 on session 15 which accounts for <u>25% of final grade</u>.

<u>Required Textbook</u>

Rue and Byars. <u>Management Theory And Application</u>. (Fifth Edition), Irwin. 1989.

Occasional Handouts by the instructor.

<u>Examination Attendance</u>

Everyone is required to take examinations on the assigned day, unless arrangements have been made with the instructor prior to that day. There are no make-up exams, and missed exams will receive the lowest "F".

-1-

COURSE OUTLINE

Session	Date	Topic	Reading
1.		Introduction	Ottaway, 1
		History of Management	2
2.		International Management	3
3.		Business Ethics	4
4.		Communications	5
		Decision-making	6
5.		Planning	7
		Strategic Management	8
6.		Organizing Work	10
		Exam I	
7.		Organizational Structure	11
		Human Resource Function	12
8.		Staffing and Development	13
		Motivation	14
9.		Motivation	14
		Leadership	15
10.		Leadership	15
		Reward Systems	16
11.		Reward Systems	16
		Exam II	
12.		Work Groups	17
		Stress Management	18
13.		Control	20
		Control	20
14.		Managing Change	19
		Managing Change	19
15.		Exam III	

GUIDELINES FOR OBSERVATIONS AT WORK

These are only suggested areas to look at in your work organization. You may apply any part of the course material you wish. If you have any questions about the observations and journal keeping, please see me. Try to make several entries each week. Keep them in a notebook.

Session 1. (Pedagogy and Mangement History) How can your work place be a learning resource for you? Are there any colleagues you want to incorporate in this exercise? Where in the history of management does your organization seem to operating?

Session 2. (International Management) Is your organization an international one? How? What type? Do any of Houghton's points apply to your organization?

Session 3. (Business Ethics) Are Friedman's ideas at home in your work organization? Do you have a code of ethics? Bring a copy.

Session 4. (Communications and Decision-making) Diagnose some miscommunications from the model of communications. Diagnose non-verbal communications. What is the difference between decision-making and problem-solving at work?

Session 5. (Planning and Strategic Management) Prepare for Exam I.

Session 6. (Organizing Work) What is the span of management in your organization? Does delegation occur? Why not, if not?

Session 7. (Organization Structure and HR Function) What form of structure does your organization have? What recruitment policy does your organization have? Are tests used?

Session 8. (Staffing and Motivation) What training programs does your organization have? Orientation? Overseas staffing? What theory of motivation is used in your organization?

Session 9. (Motivation and Leadership) Is the same theory of motivation used throughout the organization? Do American motivation and leadership theories work overseas?

Session 10. (Leadership and Rewards) Prepare for Exam II.

Session 11. (Rewards) What type of performance appraisal is used in your work organization? Is it effective?

Session 12. (Work Groups and Stress) What reference group is used in your work organization? What are the stressors of your job?

Session 13. (Control) What control methods are used in your organization? Are they different for overseas units? Prepare term paper for next time.

Session 14. (Managing Change) Prepare for Exam III.

-3-

of each chapter. The discussion period will include their presentation on the cases, as well as the workplace reports of part-time students. The second change will be that everyone will be required to write a paper on what they have learned. Thirdly, I am going to require full-time students to make site visits to classmates' workplaces and write reports on the visits.

The Case of Carl and the Concept of Socialization

Diane Gillespie, associate professor in the Goodrich Scholarship Program at the University of Nebraska at Omaha, volunteered this entry, adapted from her forthcoming book *The Minds We* (Southern Illinois Press). The work sample is a narrative account of a classroom episode that begins when a student questions Dr. Gillespie's approach to the concept of socialization. What follows are excerpts from the narrative, accompanied by reflections on its meaning and implications.

I share this story because it was a turning point in my teaching. I had always known that it was important to create bridges between my students' life experiences and the conceptual abstractions that so often intimidate them. If they can feel personally connected to the concepts and theories they study, then they can begin to feel a sense of belonging to the academic world. The diversity in my classrooms provides a reservoir of experiences from which to draw, but the multi-dimensionality can overwhelm us too. For example, sitting next to Carl was Lien, an Asian-American refugee, who, well socialized, memorized every chapter in the book (including the one on socialization). I try to get my students to stay with a new concept long enough for it to have meaning in an increasingly expanding conceptual network. Where I see a broad highway between experience and ideas,

. . . Carl's hand shot up from the back of the class, where he often sat alone, away from the other African-American students who usually sat together. The suddenness of his movement startled me. And as our eyes met, before I could even speak his name, he blurted out loudly, "All this socialization stuff is just not true -- it's all bullshit." Stunned by the directness, I remember those words exactly . . . and the way his smile covered the intensity of his feelings. The class fell silent. . . . I remember distinctly noticing his hair as he spoke out -- he had just tinted the front of it orange. Momentarily locked in his gaze, I suspected that this was his first "public" commitment to ideas -- this "socialization stuff" mattered to him deeply.

Until Carl, I had found this unit easy to teach. My mostly nontraditional students seemed to "get" socialization like the Pepsi can that drops down from the vending machine. Now behind in the syllabus, I wanted to be in the next readings, and so I had dropped the coins in the socialization slot. But there sat Carl with his newly tinted orange hair and defiant hand protesting all my tacit expectations and assumptions. . . .

As I walked back to my office [after class], I sensed that Carl's response represented more than an individual's idiosyncratic confusion and that I needed to be listening to him and maybe other students in a new way. . . . For years I had used my students' knowledge of civil rights as a bridge into courses and syllabi that excluded their perspectives. And right on through the 1970s, I tacitly held a frame of reference that originated in the 1960s. Sitting in my class fifteen years later, Carl had little experience with or knowledge of the civil rights movement. How, I asked myself, might I teach this chapter differently? A simulation? One gradually took shape in my mind. . . .

Although Carl was very engaged in the discussion that followed

my students often perceive the chasm with the flimsy footbridge in *Indiana Jones*.

Carl had resisted the concept of socialization itself in a way that I had never experienced before. In the process of reteaching it, I began to recognize how much my students' lives had changed, including their concrete experiences of socialization. As Carl heard the discussion about the simulation, he began to think about how some of his life experiences might fit socialization theory. It was not, however, just the experience that trans-

the simulation, I remember more vividly what he said after all
the students left class: All three of his brothers were in
prison and his father, an alcoholic, had left his family. He
fought theories of socialization because, as he put it, "I
thought it meant I would wind up like all the other men in my
family. I've always seen myself as an 'individualist,' but now
I see that these ideas are more complex and that things aren't
one way or the other. How do you think like this without
getting mixed up and scared?"

What I didn't apprehend then but know now, in this act of
recollection, is that, like Carl, I was scared. His actions
were essential to my development as a teacher. Looking back,
I realize it was my first serious encounter with being a
middle-aged teacher. I had lost contact with some of the
lifeworld of my students, with the backstage of our classroom.
For the first time I questioned my tacit knowledge about my
students' frames of reference and began to wonder how I would
remain connected to them as I grew older.

formed his ability to be receptive to new information; nor was it my particular method or even the particular simulation. Rather it was our ability to trust each other and to listen attentively to the other in public and private dialogues. As he began to *frame his concerns* in light of the concepts from the chapter, I more directly connected him with real, ongoing academic debates about responsibility and choice in traditional socialization.

The story reveals Carl's vulnerability as a black male in a family system where he perceives the other men to have failed. But the story also reveals my vulnerabilities as a white female teacher becoming aware of her own age. As a result of seeing this broader context, I find myself quite naturally seeking to uncover on a much more regular basis what exactly my students are thinking about when they think about "subject matter."

Computer Conferencing About Computer Languages

Elizabeth Hurley Lawrence, associate professor of science, mathematics, and technology at Empire State College, documents through a transcript of a computer conference her teaching of a course on artificial intelligence. In the course, students interacted with her and with one another through such computer conferencing. In the accompanying reflective essay she addresses the advantages and drawbacks to this approach as compared with a traditional seminar and class discussion. (Note: Students signed on with both first and last names, but last names have been deleted in this sample transcript.)

Betty Lawrence (April 21, 1991, 19:36)
"Object-Oriented Languages"
    Now that you have been reading about languages of AI,
let's discuss them a bit. Here's a question adopted from the
text: It has been noted that object-oriented languages seem
more natural to novices than to professional programmers on
their first exposure. Do you agree or disagree? Speak from
your experience.

Gary (April 22, 1991, 16:48)
    I think I would have to agree. Why? I can only guess but
after you have been programming awhile, the various higher-
level languages seem for the most part the same (except
syntactically). There are basic differences of course, but
they seem to me to be similar. With the AI languages, they are
different than the high-level structured languages (from what
little I have been exposed to). The AI languages seem to be
more loosely structured, which might also be a difficulty for
experienced programmers/software engineers to grasp. For me,
I need to get hands-on experience -- meaning, give me a
computer and the book and let me learn it. I can't just read
about it.

Forrest (April 22, 1991, 21:02)
    I agree with Gary. I've been programming in Pascal for a
few years and more recently in C. The concepts of objects,
Polymorphism, and Inheritance that are the backbone of OOP are
difficult ideas to grasp without a "hands-on" approach. I am
struggling with Object Oriented Pascal and C++ right now. . .
. It took me a while to work up enough nerve to jump in here
with something to say.

Betty Lawrence (April 22, 1991, 21:02)
    I'm glad you did, Forrest. Good response, too! Have any
of you tried to write a Prolog program? If you do, put it in
the cafeteria. I promise I'll try, too. Does anyone have
access to a compiler?

Bill (April 23, 1991, 23:06)
    I've got the DOS version of the PDC Prolog 3.2. They
resumed marketing this language when Borland dropped it. It's
not on my machine at the moment, but if I delete six or seven
meg of various games saved in progress since January of 1988,
I can make room for it.

Michael (April 25, 1991, 22:27)
    I have tried to read about and understand what the big
draw for OOP is. For me, it is hard to see where it is so much
different from writing procedures and functions and then
calling them (other than the terms you use to describe them).

1

The excerpt is from a "computer conference" offered last spring at Empire State College. Eight students participated in the conference. The activities for the course included study of a text, *Artificial Intelligence*, by Firebaugh, with answers to selected text questions sent through regular or electronic mail; participation in the computer conference over a space of four months; and completion of a final project. . . .

I am both excited and frustrated by this mode of delivery. For adults, it offers great potential for fitting education into their busy lives. They can participate when their schedules permit. They have access to other learners from around the state and, potentially, around the world. At Empire State College, our primary way of providing flexibility of schedule is through one-to-one meetings with a faculty member, so discussions among students like this one are less frequent than they should be.

On the other hand, though I have tried to liken this discussion to that which occurs around a seminar table, it is not. Body language is totally missing. I also can't look someone in the eye and call on them. I could request an answer of a particular student in the conference, but that person may not sign on for days and others may refrain from participating in the meantime. As you can see from the sample, I refrained from doing that. I did send personal messages through electronic mail, however.

Participation is a challenge — some contribute little, some

```
What type of programming applications are you trying to do
with OOP, Gary? . . .

Forrest (April 26, 1991, 1:04)
     Has anyone used or heard anything about Borland C++? I
have Turbo C++ from Borland and am wondering if it's worth
upgrading. I know that Borland C++ offers support for Windows
programmers, but I wonder what other enhancements they might
have made?

Betty Lawrence (April 28, 1991, 23:49)
     I hope someone knows the answers to these questions. I'll
see what I can find out.

Gary (May 7, 1991, 17:16)
     I believe there are applications in industry for these
programs. By the way, OOP is POOP spelled inside out. Oh well,
a little attempt at humor. I found a very interesting product
called PROCASE. It is an object-oriented database that stores
objects about your code. It keeps track of what calls what,
memory overflow, and many other things to help the software
engineer to do a better job. I don't have the literature in
front of me at present but will expand on it if anyone is
interested.

Betty Lawrence (May 7, 1991, 22:40)
     I'm interested. I've heard about these packages but have
never used one.

Paul (May 13, 1991, 12:30)
     I have had some experiences with UNIFY, which is a
Relation Database. It is very similar to Prolog and Lisp in
that it observes relationships. In UNIFY they are called
explicit Relationships. Most tables are linked together by Key
Fields with Parent and Child connectivity. I found using this
was much easier than teaching myself C.

Paul (May 14, 1991, 12:52)
     I meant to say Unify is a Relational Database.
```

2

too much. This, however, is not unlike the situation in a seminar. Some students are initially uncomfortable with their contributions being exhibited so openly in written form, and it does take some time to adjust to this new mode. Some are long-winded and it is hard to follow messages more than one screen long. But, the benefits far outweigh the challenges. The sharing of expertise is rich and not available through any textbook.

For me, it is a freeing and humbling experience. Other than setting up the items and commenting briefly or sometimes redirecting a conversation, I have little control over what occurs here. I have to trust that the students will engage in serious dialogue and will respect one another's views. The sample shows that they certainly did. In other uses of this mode around the college, we have found this generally to be the case.

Experimenting With the Evaluation of Student Work

William R. Whipple is associate dean for academic affairs at Albright College. His entry focuses on a course he taught at the University of Maine while the director of the honors program and associate professor of psychology. Excerpted from a longer entry that takes up issues of course planning and design, the work sample and reflections that follow look particularly at Dr. Whipple's changing practice in the area of evaluating student work.

Original

PSYCHOLOGY OF MOTIVATION
Spring, 1989 semester

Instructor: Dr. William R. Whipple   office: Thomson Honors Center

Office hours: by appointment -- see me after class or call ext. 3263.

In this course we will explore the concept of motivation from a variety of psychological perspectives: physiological, behavioral, cognitive, and social. Text for the course is Motivation by Herbert Petri (2nd ed.). We will read all of this book except for chapters 9 and 14. In addition, we will read some other materials dealing with operant approaches to motivation (choice, matching, and preference reversal), which are not covered in Petri's book; these materials will be handed out in class. It is very important that you read the assigned chapters before the date on which they are listed in the schedule below. Discussions in class will not duplicate the readings but will assume that you are familiar with the relevant sections of the text. You will also probably find it necessary to re-read portions of the text after the class discussion.

I do not take attendance in class, but because of the way in which I assess your learning (see below) you will find it necessary to come to class all the time. Our exploration of motivation will involve a great deal of open discussion during class, and it will be impossible to make this up if you are absent. I suggest that you resolve never to miss a class unless you are honestly too ill to come. I also suggest that you keep this resolution.

Exams: You will find my exams very unusual. At first, they may annoy you; however, once you become used to the format, I think you will find them interesting and even fun. Each exam will contain two or three essay questions. The answers to these questions will not be found in the book; indeed, in many cases the answers are not known. The point of the test is not to get the correct answer, but to show that you know how to go about solving a problem. In doing so, you will get to use (rather than merely parrot) the material we have been studying. It is impossible to cram for my tests; it is also virtually impossible to cheat. In fact, you will be required to discuss the questions with other students. (However, you must write your own answers.)

There will be three tests, plus a practice test early in the course. The practice test (Exam 0) does not count toward your grade; it is for the purpose of helping you to get used to the nature of my exams. Each of the other three exams accounts for 25% of your final grade. The remaining 25% will be the higher of (1) the average score on Exams 1-3 of the students in your exam group OR (2) your score on the optional final exam. The final exam may also be used to substitute for any tests missed because of illness.

Grading practices: I do not grade on a curve. It is always my hope, at the beginning of a semester, that everybody in the class will understand the material so fully that I can honestly give everybody an A. This hasn't happened yet, but maybe it will this time. Three things will help you to improve your grade: (1) do the reading, on time; (2) come to class, always; and (3) spend a lot of time thinking about the concepts which we are discussing -- look for examples of them in everyday life and think to yourself how you would explain these examples.

I n the spring of 1989, I taught an upper-level psychology course on motivation. While the topics covered were quite traditional, I used the course to experiment with a new method of student evaluation. In place of objective exams, students wrote essays based on open-ended questions requiring both understanding of the theories and the ability to synthesize ideas in a creative fashion. The class was divided into "exam groups" of five to six students, and when the exam question was handed out in class, the students broke up into these groups to discuss the question and share their ideas. They then took the question home. Further consultation within (or even between) groups outside of class was permitted, but students were required to write their own papers without looking at what anyone else had written. The essays were evaluated using a customized feedback sheet, which I handed out with the test so that students would know what was expected of them. Because of the unfamiliarity of the procedure, students were told that the first of these tests was for practice and would not count toward their course grade. Students' grades were based primarily on their own work, but, as indicated in the syllabus, a small component of the grade was also based on the performance of their group, to encourage cooperation rather than competition.

Toward the end of the semester I concluded that the class, while fairly successful, needed further development (a point confirmed by students' course evaluations). I therefore asked one of the top students from the class to work with me over the summer to revise it and to serve as an undergraduate teaching assistant when the course was next offered. She agreed, and we met weekly throughout the summer to modify and improve the course.

Student course ratings

Revision

included several points relevant to the grading and evaluation of student work:

1. The unorthodox testing method was appreciated, although — despite the practice exam and the detailed evaluation sheets — students still felt they had little control over their grades.

2. Students reported that they learned more in the group discussions than from either class lectures or reading. However some groups were much more effective than others; students in marginally functional groups felt cheated out of some of the learning that they had expected.

3. Overall, the course had too little structure for most students; they thought more predictability and regularity would improve their learning and performance on assignments.

In response to these points, my student colleague and I made a number of changes in the area of the evaluation of student work.

In our revision, we continued the evaluation of student essays written after group discussion, but the number of discussions/papers was expanded from three to nine. Each student was assigned to three different groups over the semester, in each group completing one exam and two shorter group projects. This

Original

```
                          Psych 351 — Motivation
                            Practice Exam #1


Intraspecific aggression in humans is thought by many ethologists to be
innate, while psychologists (predictably) tend to emphasize to a greater
extent the role of learning in aggression.

Considering what you have read, and the topics we have discussed in class,
work out the best possible argument for an innate component to human aggression,
and the best argument for a learned component.  Use real-life observations
of human behavior to illustrate your arguments.  Can you think of an
experiment which would prove that there is an innate component to human
aggression?  If so, describe it and explain as well as possible what the
component is.
```

increased the amount of time devoted to group work (which appeared to be the most potent learning situation) and also prevented any individual student from being stranded in a dysfunctional group.

Furthermore, the class became more structured overall. The outline was more detailed and we adhered to it more closely. A detailed explanation of the course procedures and the ways they differed from those of other courses was passed out and discussed on the first day. Evaluation of all essays was based on a four-dimensional scale (A, D, I, C), which was identical for all written work (see enclosed materials). Finally, the initial handout explained the percentages by which each dimension contributed to the final grade.

How successful were these changes? Student evaluations of the revised course suggest that many of our original concerns were eliminated in the new version of the course. In particular, discomfort about grading procedures was substantially reduced. Indeed, some students reported a curious indifference to their grades, as though their motivation regarding this course had shifted from an extrinsic to an intrinsic basis. The fact that students wrote and received grades on nine essays — as

Revision

```
                    PSYCH 351 (Motivation)

               Group Project #1    due Feb. 2, 1990

     After discussing both sides of the issue in your groups, write a brief
     statement defending either (1) the notion that aggression is innate in humans
     OR (2) the idea that aggression is not innate in humans.  Your answer should
     explain WHY you take the position you do, citing evidence which you think
     would be convincing to a disinterested outsider.  You should also consider the
     arguments of the opposing side, and indicate why you reject these.

     A few sentences (about 1 side of a page if you type or write in small
     handwriting) should be sufficient for a good, concise response.


     Evaluation

     In evaluating both this and the other written work that you submit, the
     following factors will be taken into account -- in roughly equal proportions:

         A - Accuracy:          Do your factual claims correctly reflect the
                                data?  When you refer to another writer's
                                position, do you present it as s/he would do?
                                Are your facts precise?

         D - Depth:             Have you explored the question beyond superficial
                                levels?  Do you see connections which were not
                                spelled out in the readings or lectures?  Do you
                                ask probing questions?

         I - Imagination:       Do you relate what you are studying to real life?
                                Are your examples interesting and appropriate?
                                Do you take a creative approach to explaining
                                your point?  (Note: Creativity is a virtue in the
                                presentation of theories or the interpretation of
                                data.  Creativity in the presentation of data is
                                much less praiseworthy.  Imagine all the theories
                                you like, but don't make up your data.)

         C - Clarity:           Is your paper well written and easy to
                                understand?  Do you use the English language with
                                skill and precision?  Can you be both brief and
                                clear in your explanation?
```

opposed to three the previous year — might also have helped to increase students' confidence in the grading system. Most students applauded the extensive use of groups and the evaluation methods.

On a slightly different note, I want to add that the process of collaborating with a student in both the design and teaching of the course had beneficial effects on my teaching style that go beyond this particular class. As we worked together, I became increasingly aware of the fact that my loosely structured and abstract style of thinking can cause confusion for students, particularly those whose own styles are more linear and concrete. It was fortunate that the student with whom I was working is a very concrete thinker; the accommodations both of us made in order to understand each other gave us very deep insights into a different manner of approaching knowledge. If my classroom discussion of a topic became too abstruse, she would interject by saying, "Let's think of an example here." In addition to making the concepts in the motivation course more accessible to students, her interjections alerted me to a need continually to monitor the degree of abstraction with which I teach in other classroom situations. That, perhaps, will be the most far-reaching outcome of this course-development project.

Helping Students Write About History

James Wilkinson, history teacher and director of the Derek Bok Center for Teaching and Learning at Harvard, submitted this entry, which is presented here in its entirety. The work sample consists of a student's short, typed book review, showing the feedback Dr. Wilkinson offered that student. In his reflective statement, Dr. Wilkinson explains why he wrote the comments he did, and reflects on what these comments reveal about the way he tends to respond to student writing.

This paper was submitted as the second of three required book reports in my course, History 134, "Germany in the Twentieth Century." The student, John Pickering, is a junior history major. He received a *B* on his first paper, which had some good ideas but lacked even the most elementary organization. I was delighted that for his second effort John managed to write more clearly — using topic sentences and trying to fashion a sustained argument. I was especially concerned that he recognize that he was on the right track, and therefore I did not criticize the order in which he made his points beyond pointing out that the final one should have come first.

Of greater concern to me at this point in the semester was the fact that John was not offering very much evidence to support his views. It seemed to me (though I did not say so) that the effort to organize his thoughts had so completely absorbed him that he had neglected to pay adequate attention to justifying them. Thus, in addition to some comment on organization, I chose to focus principally on the absence of evidence, both in my marginal comments and in my overall assessment at the end of the paper. In fact, John's final book report did include more factual evidence, and received a grade of *A-*.

I believe that his paper is slightly better than the average paper I received in the course. But that did not mean I was reluctant to push him to do better. On the contrary, it is the bright students who frequently

---

John Pickering
History 134
December 3, 1990

Book Report on Peter Gay's <u>Weimar Culture</u>

Peter Gay's <u>Weimar Culture: The Outsider as Insider</u>, was published in 1968. It is a short book dealing with a complex topic. In fact, the cultural history of the Weimar years is so complex that it seems to me that Peter Gay would have done better to choose a more narrow focus and say more about it. But perhaps he wanted to give an overview and leave the details to other authors. At any rate, <u>Weimar Culture</u> tries to say a lot in its 200 pages, and is only partially successful.

The main problem with the book, from my point of view, is that it assumes that the reader is already familiar with Weimar history, which may not be the case, at least for beginning students of the period. It is true that Gay includes what can best be termed a "crash course" in Weimar history in an appendix (pp. 147-164). But it would be more useful to weave the political history in better with the cultural history. For example, when Gay writes about youth movements and their neoramantic outlook on the chapter entitled "The Hunger for Wholeness" (pp. 70-101), he might have tied this topic to the economy of Germany at the time. Upheavals in the German economy such as the inflation of 1923 and the burden of reparations payments must have had a depressing effect on the outlook of German young people, just as the prospect of a recession has a depressing effect on college students today. I think that Gay missed an opportunity here to link politics and culture, which he should have grasped.

[Marginal handwritten notes:]
Is this first sentence really relevant to your argument?
Why is this not an appropriate assumption?
Good example
Why do you say this? Do you have any evidence? Does Gay present any?

Excellent point {margin note}

    The other problem with Peter Gay's view of Weimar culture
is that he makes everything come out too neatly in the end. There
is a sense that the doom of Weimar culture is preordained; the brave
beginnings, we know, will end in disaster. Gay does not try to put
himself in the shoes of Weimar thinkers and poets, who had no way of
knowing how things would turn out, as we do today. Perhaps if Gay
had quoted more from diaries, or else given more air time for writers
who were enthusiastic about the Weimar Republic, he would have avoided
giving the impression that everything was over before it begun. The
heavy tramp of Nazi jackboots resounds from his pages. I do not think
this is an accurate description of Weimar atmospherics.

This seems a bit too over-dramatic. {margin note}

    Finally, I have problems with the theme that Gay keeps pushing
about the outsiders as insiders. The so-called "outsiders" before
World War I -- writers, artists, thinkers -- suddenly become "insiders"
after 1918. At least that is what Gay wants us to think. But these
people were never really insiders, or else they could not have been
pushed out so fast when the Weimar regime ran into trouble with the
Depression of 1929. It seems to me that the real insiders -- judges,
bureaucrats, police -- stayed as insiders all along, and when the
Nazis came to power they just clamped down on culture they had hated
all along.

Again, what evidence do we have? {margin note}

B+ {circled}

John – A nice job overall. I think you could have
reordered the paragraphs in order to deal with Gay's
principal thesis (what you term "the theme that
Gay keeps pushing") first. I also think you needed
more direct quotes from the book as evidence to
support your points. It's a very negative review —
don't you have anything good to say about Gay?
on the other hand, it's thoughtful, clear, and well written

---

are not challenged sufficiently here and who therefore need someone to point out what they could do better. At the same time, there is nothing to be gained from raising too many points at once — better, I feel, to concentrate on one or two at a time. Thus my feeling was that John, having begun to come to grips with his problem of poor organization, was now ready to devote some thought to the problem of evidence but should not have to contend with other issues (such as the problem of Gay's intended audience) in more than a passing manner.

What these comments indicate about my response to student writing, I believe, is first that I offer encouragement, even where there is room for improvement, and second that I am very specific about what I want students to do to improve without being too confining. That is, I do not write out what they should have said, but instead give them general guidelines, which I find to be the most helpful in improving their writing.

Contributing to (and Learning From) a Videoconference on Dating Violence

This entry was volunteered by Arthur Chickering, University Professor at George Mason University and an expert in student development; it focuses on his participation in the national teleconference panel "Dating Violence: Issues for Campus Management." The work sample consists of excerpts from his "prompt notes," which include his general propositions, some suggested interventions, and quotes from women who have experienced dating violence. In his accompanying reflection, he describes how he prepared for the teleconference and the effect of his participation on his teaching.

M y role in the tele-conference was to apply my expertise on student development in college to this problem area. I said that I knew little about dating violence but that I would be willing to participate. . . .

To prepare, I reviewed a fat stack of literature on dating violence. I met with Ron Campbell, housing director here at GMU who has been working with "men's groups" on this topic, who shared his experiences and supplied additional reading. I next turned to the key developmental theories we examine in my "Adult Development and Learning" course. . . . I found that, indeed, perspectives from developmental theory not only shed light on dating violence "offenders" and "victims" but also had implications for intervention.

Based on this review, I suggested topic areas and pertinent literature for conference-planning purposes, and took principal responsibility for those aspects of the conference that dealt with student-development issues and campus interventions to encourage

development. . . .

Soon I received a tape of interview segments from female "victims." These "flesh-and-blood" segments gave revealing clues to their developmental stages and to the developmental areas where they were still immature. Now I could tie my general concepts concerning student development to these live materials.

I next prepared my "Prompt Notes."

After the teleconference, the studio audience was positive about the useful concepts and concrete interventions. They were both interested and entertained. . . .

I believe this experience made significant contributions to my teaching. Developmental stage theories are the most important and difficult content in my "Adult Development and Learning" course. Many students also have difficulty seeing

```
developmental growth toward the conscientious stage of ego
development, commitments in relativism, and procedural knowing, as
well as increased impulse control, sex role clarification, and the
capacity for intimacy.

Pertinent Developmental Theories

Loevinger, Stages of Ego Development:

                    Impulse Control     Interpersonal      Cognitive
                    Character Development   Style            Style

Self-Protective     Externalizing blame  Wary, manipul-    Conceptual
Opportunistic       Opportunistic        lative, exploi-   Simplicity
                                         tative

Conformist          Conformity to ex-    Belonging         Stereotypes
                    ternal rules;        Superficial       Cliches
                    Guilt for breaking   niceness
                    rule

Conscientious       Self-evaluated       Intensive,        Conceptual
                    standards; self-     Responsible,      Complexity
                    criticism; guilt     Mutual, Con-
                    for consequences;    cern for
                    long term goals      communication
                    and ideals

Segment quotes:

"He'd always had a bad temper. The best way to get his way was to
throw a temper tantrum."

"He got mad at me because I cut my hair. He said 'How could he be
seen with me.'"

"He says what you're going to wear, who you're going to see, what
groups you're going to be in.
"He pinned me down on the floor. I was calling for help. HIs
roommates were there and didn't do anything.

"I'm trying to gain my own identity."

"The best signals are possessiveness. He treats you like you're his
property."

Perry, Positions of Ethical and Intellectual Development

Dualistic: Established authorities define right and wrong. The
           legitimacy of alternative perspectives is not established.

Multiplicity: Anyone has a right to own opinion. Where authorities
              don't know the right answers... no one is wrong.
Points            of view are equally valid, not subject to
```

how these concepts help one to understand and act on "real life" issues concerning college and university policies, student personnel services activities, curricula content, and teaching practices. Working this teleconference taught me about an arena for application where these concepts have significant power. Many students have been involved in dating violence, either as offenders or as victims or through the experiences of close friends, so they can connect with their own experiences.

The teleconference segments that show victims of dating violence are particularly powerful in the classroom. They supply emotionally charged human experiences pertinent to the concepts and their applicability. I can ask student subgroups to make their own judgments about the developmental stages and developmental tasks of the interviewees. These shared reflections can help expose the strengths and limitations of the theories. Then I can ask students to propose interventions consistent with the theories and with the students' developmental status. I can conclude by asking students to critique the theory presentations and the suggested interventions given throughout the full tape.

I look forward to modifying my course design to use these materials. But the proof of the pudding will be in the implementation. Stay tuned.

Learning About Student Writing Strategies

Assistant professor Jennifer Hicks conducted research on the effects of collaborative writing on the individual writing styles of students in her developmental writing courses at Massachusetts Bay Community College. To determine these effects, she used Classroom Research methods: For each assignment, students completed a "process self-analysis" (a record of the steps taken and the amount of time spent on each step in the writing process) and during the first and last weeks of the course they completed a questionnaire about their revision strategies. Significant changes were found, as indicated in the work sample: a tally sheet from a questionnaire completed by students. The reflective portion of the entry is excerpted from a written report on the research Prof. Hicks presented at a conference on teaching and learning in the spring of 1991; a complete version of that report appears in the Fall 1991 *The Educational Forum: A Journal of Teaching, Learning, and Professional Development* (Vol. 2, Massachusetts Bay Community College).

Appendix 4.
Revision Habit Questionnaire Findings

		intial # of respondents	terminal # of respondents
1.	definition of revise		
	vague ("fix" or "make better")	9	1
	check for mechanical errors	11	5
	check structure	0	5
	add/delete content	2	19
	check clarity	1	16
2.	steps of revision		
	mechanics only	13	0
	mechanics then structure	6	0
	mechanics then content	3	3
	content then structure then mechanics	1	6
	content then mechanic then structure	0	14
3.	not applicable to academic writing		
4.	changes made in academic work		
	content	14	22
	add information	11	19
	delete information	6	9
	sentence structure	16	10
	paragraph order	9	10
	punctuation	12	6
	spelling	14	13
	tone	4	8
	word choice	18	13
	other	0	0
5.	when changes are made		
	immediately, before going on	14	4
	while re-reading, before finished	3	10
	while re-reading, after finished	6	9
6.	no applicable answers		

15

There was a 100% increase in revision between the first and third papers, indicating that, indeed, the knowledge and use of revision was becoming part of the students' writing process. . . . The number of reported steps in mid-writing rose more than 70%, with "have someone read my paper" accounting for all the increased responses. The question is whether the collaborative writing itself led to this. . . .

Now, at the end of the project, I realize that my research question — Will writing a group paper help students become better individual writers? — probably wasn't the best. If I take the question at face value, the answer would have to be no. Students don't tend to become better individual writers if they are urged to be collaborative writers. I have no documentation that supports the idea that the writing of the group paper and exposure to various writing processes within the group, *in and of itself*, made the students better writers. Yet, the fact remains that all the students did improve. They all left the course with a greater understanding of revision and audience, and they left with the knowledge of how to use this information to their advantage in their writing. But, if I can't claim the improvement was caused by writing the collaborative paper, what was it caused by? . . .

I would like to think that some important realization happened because of this project. I would like categorically to state that understanding the process is essential to good writing. Yet, I have other classes where students keep wonderful process journals that demon-

7.	when does re-reading occur*[2]		
	after each sentence	9	2
	after each paragraph	10	10
	when finished	11	23
8.	no applicable answers		
9.	see 5		
	no discernible differences from 5		
10.	changing mind while writing		
	yes, go with new idea, throw old away	5	8
	yes, stick with old idea	8	2
	no	10	5
11.	audience		
	self	11	0[3]
	peers	2	0
	teacher	3	5
	school	6	0
	"the audience"	1	18

12. 13, 14, 15 not applicable to project

---

[2] Totals equal more than 23 because of answers like: "I re-read all the time. After every sentence, paragraph, and when I'm done."

[3] The significant change here is probably attributable to the change in verbal directions to complete the questionnaire. The second time it was administered, I asked them to fill it out based on what they got out of this class.

16

---

strate their understanding of the writing process, but they write only average papers. So apparently, one needs more than just an understanding of the process to be a good writer. I would like to say that writing a paper as a group enabled students to pick and choose among a variety of writing processes and refine one or more for their own use. But I don't know that this happened. I would like to say that my particular sequencing of assignments is imperative to improving writing ability. But I used a different sequence in a different class and the results were just as good. . . . Apparently, then, I can't draw a generalized conclusion from this project.

And, that's what Classroom Research is. Rather than finding an answer to world hunger, Classroom Research merely feeds a particular class. . . . I've learned to recognize the importance of looking at a class as a group of individuals able to teach me a great deal about themselves at a particular point in time.

Chapter 4

Portfolios on Your Campus: Getting Started

As we've argued in previous chapters, the teaching portfolio is no one thing; it's a tool, a technology, to be used in ways that advance particular purposes. Its structure and format, the array of entries included in it, the processes it entails, and the methods by which it is judged will depend on institutional (and perhaps departmental) context and culture. Nevertheless, campuses looking to introduce portfolios can learn relevant lessons from current practice.

Finding the Right Purposes and Occasions

Many of the campuses that have gotten involved in teaching portfolios have done so — in the words of one practitioner — to "tilt the balance" between research and teaching, to change the rules of promotion and tenure decision making. That's a right idea, of course, and one that some campuses might be ready to tackle. At Syracuse University, for instance, portfolios are a piece of a larger, longer-term effort to shift reward structures toward teaching. As part of its Focus on Teaching project, a number of schools and colleges at Syracuse require faculty to submit a range of materials within a portfolio as part of revised promotion and tenure procedures.

On campuses where such groundwork has yet to be laid, however, high-stakes occasions might not be the place to start. Indeed, a potential danger at this early stage in the development of teaching portfolios lies in the rush to attach them to reward systems and tenure. Such a high-stakes context can in fact work against some of their strengths, washing out rich detail and variety for the sake of more uniform and efficient decision making. On the other hand, where nothing at all is at stake, portfolios are likely to become an empty exercise.

A middle ground makes sense to us as a place to start: one where the context is indeed evaluative — where judgments that people care about are being made — but where the stakes are not so high as to subvert the evolving character of the teaching portfolio itself.

Campuses beginning a portfolio project might, for instance, think of using portfolios for the selection of teaching-award winners. This is a route recently taken by University College of the University of Maryland. Nominees for teaching-excellence awards assemble and submit an extensive portfolio, which is reviewed and evaluated by a five-member student/faculty committee. Contents of the portfolio vary, but (in keeping with the category of "actual teaching") nominees in the coming academic year will be asked to include a "live from the classroom" videotape.

Similarly, the University of Pittsburgh now employs teaching portfolios to select recipients of its President's Distinguished Teacher Award. Last year, a selection committee of eight distinguished faculty members and two students evaluated dossiers that included a summary of teaching responsibilities, a statement of teaching goals, annotated instructional materials from two settings, student and peer evaluations, and a description of activities aimed at improved teaching.

A similarly "medium-stakes" occasion is teaching-assistant training, where some interest in the teaching portfolio has begun to emerge — at Harvard's Derek Bok Center for Teaching and Learning, for instance, where director James Wilkinson has begun working with teaching assistants to develop portfolios. The purpose of the activity is, first and foremost, teaching improvement; portfolios give TAs a vehicle for stepping back from their classroom experience, putting the pieces together, strategizing about needed improvements. As they complete their graduate

49

work, the resulting documentation of their teaching effectiveness — evidence they can put in the hands of prospective employers — is a further benefit. But beyond the benefit to individual TAs, there's an institutional payoff from teaching portfolios at Harvard: Professors teaching huge lecture courses, with twenty or thirty discussion sections, will be able to use portfolios more thoughtfully to select TAs to run those sections.

TA training and teaching-award competitions are just two occasions where teaching portfolios might be productively introduced; merit awards, sabbatical proposals, third-year reviews, and small-grant competitions have also been suggested. Doubtless there are other occasions. The important point is to situate portfolio projects in contexts where decisions that people care about are being made; where bureaucracy doesn't overwhelm substance; where trial and error and thoughtful invention have a chance; and — the point we continue to return to — where there's a real interest in using the portfolio to get at the complexities of exemplary teaching.

Involving the Right People

If teaching portfolios are to catch on, the initiative must involve the institution's most respected faculty from the outset. This means on the one hand the best *teachers*: those whose portfolios will be richest, most revealing of exemplary practice, *and* most likely to get other faculty excited by the prospect of putting together their own portfolios.

But there's an argument, too, for starting with admired teachers who are also prominent *researchers*. Doing so makes a powerful statement about the value placed on the process by faculty whose status is certain and who will "go public" with the scholarship of their teaching.

Learning From the Process

One of the key lessons of the student assessment movement is that the *processes* prompted by assessment — the questions it raises, the reflection and conversation it provokes — can have more power for improvement than any

resulting data, though data are what people *initially* think will matter most. Judging from practice thus far, the same might be true when it comes to teaching portfolios.

Last spring, for instance, AAHE asked a faculty member at Alverno College to develop a sample teaching portfolio entry based on his syllabus for an introductory-level philosophy course. (You'll find Tim Riordan's entry among those in the Sample Entries section.) "This doesn't need to be a major project," we reassured him. "If you'd just spend an afternoon jotting down a few notes about how your syllabus has changed. . . ." Three weeks later he called to say that ho'd "gotten kind of caught up" in the task; that the exercise of looking back and putting on paper the thinking behind evolving versions of the syllabus had been extremely thought-provoking — so much so that he changed the syllabus once again and would teach the course differently next time!

The power of the portfolio process is confirmed, too, by biology teachers participating in the Stanford Teacher Assessment Project. Interviews with the biologists indicated that the process was valuable because "(1) someone was very interested and concerned about their teaching; (2) the portfolio captured evidence that *looked like* their teaching; and (3) selecting evidence and writing captions and reflections had impelled them to clarify their intentions and beliefs about students, about biology, and about teaching" (Collins 1991).

There are important lessons here for those who are trying to get a portfolio project started on their own campus. Particularly in the early stage of practice, portfolios are time-consuming and anxiety-provoking; it's not easy to look one's own teaching in the eye. Portfolio-makers need care, coaching, and time; a high emphasis on portfolio preparation, and lessened emphasis on portfolio review, might be the ticket for greatest benefits from the process.

Encouraging Collaboration

An issue that inevitably arises in the development of portfolios is whether they should be solo performances or coached and collegial. Kenneth Wolf weighs in on this point:

One of the drawbacks of portfolios is the difficulty of ensuring that the work presented is entirely that of the person whose name is on the folder. But this potential stumbling block can be turned into a stepping stone.

Instead of treating authorship as a problem, treat collaboration as a virtue. In this view, teachers would be expected to seek out the assistance of others in their teaching and in constructing their portfolios. (p. 18)

As Lee Shulman has pointed out, the dissertation — that long-standing door to academic respectability — is a coached performance (AAHE Assessment Conference address, June 1991). To treat teaching (and the development of the teaching portfolio) as a coached, collaborative activity is not to demean or undercut it but to raise its value and sharpen its practice. Again, with high-stakes decisions out of the picture — with portfolio judgment a lessened emphasis and with fuller attention to enriching the process of portfolio preparation — collaborative work is the very thing to encourage.

What's the best way to encourage collaboration? Again, the answer will depend on context, but one that occurs to us entails a sort of "buddy system" (rather like that in the New Jersey Master Faculty Program) wherein two faculty pair up for a semester to visit each other's classes; interview each other's students; confer on syllabi, exercises, and exams; then assist each other in putting together appropriate materials to document their teaching. Another powerful arrangement would be one based on mentoring, where the more experienced faculty member works with a younger colleague to organize and present appropriate work samples and reflections. Indeed, one of the reviewers of this monograph argues that developing a teaching portfolio is an ideal way to establish long-term, positive working relationships between senior and new faculty members.

Another promising route to collaboration is to house portfolio projects within departments, where conversations about teaching can be grounded in the discipline. At the University of

Nebraska, for instance, portfolios are being implemented within several very different programs, including English and agronomy, providing faculty in those units with occasions for enlarged, richer conversations about teaching. Similarly, in the education department at Otterbein College, all faculty assemble portfolios as part of their annual contract process; the department has noted a resulting increase in discussions about teaching methods, curriculum, course revision.

To foster further attention to department-level teaching concerns, one might, say, hold a departmental retreat where fifteen portfolios are passed around and discussed, with an eye not only to individual practice but to broader issues of consistency, common purpose, curricular coherence, and the power of alternative teaching methods. Held up against the usual discussions of teaching load and travel funds, it's a suggestive scenario! Over the longer term, portfolios might help departments move toward a culture of teaching, in which habits of classroom visitation, mentoring, and the like can flourish.

Teaching tends to be a private, solitary activity; collaboratively designed portfolios are an antidote to this isolation and a way to promote collegial exchange focused on the substance — the scholarship — of teaching.

Evaluating Portfolios

In November of 1990, AAHE brought together a group of twenty-five faculty and administrators using or planning to use portfolios on their own campuses; in preparation for the meeting, we asked them what issues were most on their minds. Not very surprisingly, the most frequently noted issues were those of evaluation: Who should evaluate portfolios? According to what criteria? Where would those criteria come from? Would a "scoring system" be useful? Do-able? What about reliability and validity? Where could one turn for help in this area?

The reality is that most campuses undertaking portfolios have not gotten to these questions. It's clear, however, that issues of evaluation need to be thought about, broadly aired, and planned for early on.

One source of assistance here, once again, is the work of the Stanford Teacher Assessment Project, from which two potentially useful lessons about evaluation can be drawn.

The first (mentioned earlier) is that portfolio raters are able to score portfolios after looking at only a few entries per category; anything beyond that, in the Stanford experiments, proved redundant. Collins counsels, "Ask: What will be added to the description of the knowledge, skills, and dispositions of a teacher by adding this entry?" If the answer is nothing, don't add it. Faculty are quite naturally apprehensive about the time commitment entailed in the evaluation of portfolios, but actual experience can prove this to be less of a problem than anticipated.

A second lesson from Stanford is that holistic evaluation can be more helpful than a fine-grained, analytic scoring system — a system that was found to turn the evaluation of portfolios into a mechanical task. What one wants, that is, is not a mess of scales and subscores and chicken scratches but thoughtful judgments about teaching performance as a whole. To the point here, faculty who teach writing often have considerable experience with holistic forms of scoring (and, for that matter, with student portfolios); they might be particularly helpful when it comes to the evaluation of teaching portfolios.

What else can be said about evaluation? Perhaps the most useful perspective at this point — short of extensive campus practice with portfolios — is that purposes should drive practice. That is, depending on what a campus hopes to accomplish, it might choose quite different approaches to evaluation.

If, for instance, the point is to encourage conversation about teaching across departments that are usually isolated from one another, it would make sense to have an interdisciplinary faculty group-read portfolios — portfolios that themselves represent teaching in a variety of disciplines. If, on the other hand, the point is to encourage greater attention to the content-specific nature of teaching (Shulman's "pedagogy of substance"), each department might be responsible for reviewing its own portfolios; it's notable here that a group of economists is likely to read

an entry on the teaching of supply and demand quite differently from an interdisciplinary group.

If the primary thrust of portfolios is individual improvement, the most powerful context for evaluation might be small groups or pairs of faculty. In the "buddy system" noted above, for instance, the development of portfolios might well be indistinguishable from their evaluation, which would be ongoing and highly formative.

At the other end of the continuum — high-stakes evaluation for promotion and tenure — the campus might well want to cultivate a small group of highly trained portfolio readers, individuals who specialize in particular types of entries or categories rather than being responsible for rating entire portfolios. Such an arrangement would allow for the kinds of reliability checks that faculty with careers on the line would naturally want to see.

We mean these strategies to be suggestive, of course, not exhaustive; there are no doubt *many* useful routes to evaluating portfolios. A good, final point to have in mind is, if you will, an ethical one: that no important decision about an individual should be made on the basis of a single rating or piece of evidence. No portfolio, no matter how carefully evaluated, will ever tell the whole story.

Using Portfolio Evaluation as an Occasion for Standard Setting

One of the unanswered questions about portfolio evaluation is this: What criteria should be applied in reviewing them? What are the standards against which they should be judged? What, after all, do we mean by "excellent teaching"? Obviously, there are no off-the-shelf answers to these questions. The first point to be made is that these are *good* questions, just the ones a campus that takes teaching seriously would want in the air. We believe that teaching portfolios, and especially their reading and review, can help raise those questions.

How might this be done? One option is to proceed deductively. That is, at the outset of a project to implement portfolios, a group of faculty might come together and devise "standards for good teaching" for use in evaluating finished portfolios. This strikes us as a tricky route, one in which standards might quickly become disconnected from the particulars of teaching and therefore from its reality; the result might be alarmingly bloodless (and boring). But we note that the experience at Miami-Dade Community College is quite to the contrary. There, faculty *and* students engaged in an extensive exercise to describe teaching effectiveness; their description is lively and dynamic, and does seem apt for use in evaluating portfolios.

Alternatively, standards might be derived inductively. Imagine a project in which the ten most respected teachers on campus prepared portfolios; their portfolios could be powerful grist for a faculty discussion of what good teaching "looks like." A departmental retreat with a set of members' teaching portfolios on the table, a division-wide gathering in which five faculty present their portfolios . . . occasions like these might ground and situate discussions of teaching quality and improvement.

Of course there's a third alternative as well, which is also the one we suspect most campuses will come to: a mix of these two approaches. Many campuses will have some existing statement about teaching effectiveness (in promotion criteria, for instance), and portfolios will be an occasion to consult that statement. Once faculty begin developing their portfolios, however, a need for clearer, more precise standards might become evident; new standards can be posited, their usefulness tested on completed portfolios, revisions and clarifications made. . . . What one wants, ultimately, is a collective awareness on campus that there *are*, in fact, teaching standards that people are expected to meet. It's important to say, too, (though not the subject of this monograph and not one we'll expand on) that there need to be

resources and expertise to help faculty move their performance toward meeting such standards.

Establishing a Spirit of Experimentation

Portfolios are in an early stage of development; difficult questions lie before us. Campuses seeking to implement portfolios would do well to operate in a "pilot" mode, building in chances to take stock, make adjustments, and ask "how can we make teaching portfolios work better here on our campus?"

There are questions, particularly, about how the portfolio can be adapted to particular institutional settings and purposes. One can learn from but not necessarily replicate what works on another campus; each campus must find its own way. What makes sense at the University of Nebraska might seem downright silly at Gordon College; a portfolio in physics will almost certainly look quite different from a portfolio in history. Much more needs to be known about contexts and cultures.

Experimentation with additional models is also needed. This monograph looks closely at one possible model of the teaching portfolio, but in next stages of work we need several models — models that are congenial to a variety of purposes but have in common the power to capture what faculty know about teaching.

Most of all, perhaps, in this initial, experimental stage of practice, we need to keep purposes in view. Teaching portfolios could easily become "pack-ratting run rampant," an exercise in collecting paper, a dreary bureaucratic routine. Only where a view of teaching itself is at the center will teaching portfolios fulfill their special promises and help make teaching a more exciting, intellectually engaging, and public activity.

Chapter 5

Portfolios, Peer Review & the Culture of Professionalism

Throughout this monograph, we have gone out of our way to present the teaching portfolio as a tool uniquely suited to capturing some of the more complex and subtle dimensions of teaching. Portfolios that are designed and used with this end in mind, we have argued, can become vehicles through which the faculty can carry on a more professional discourse about teaching. In closing, we wish to explain why the effort to deepen and enrich the professional discourse about teaching is itself a goal worthy of our time and effort.

The story comes to mind of a man who came upon two medieval stonecutters and asked each what he was doing. The first said, "I'm squaring this bloody stone." The second looked up and said, "I'm building a cathedral." Both were doing precisely the same job. But the second had a vision of the larger whole to which he was contributing. And what a difference this made!

The cathedrals that need to be built — or more precisely, *restored* — are the academic fields and disciplines that provide intellectual homes for most of the faculty in higher education. Faculty look to their campus for guidance, rewards, and recognition; but they look also, and often with more concern, to the faculty who are members of their own scholarly community. To be recognized and respected by one's professional peers is the ultimate "reward" in academe.

This is why the call for a broader view of scholarship that we discussed in Chapter One is so important. If the academic work we call "teaching" and "service" is viewed as something that is *separate from* and *outside* the boundary of what these scholarly communities care about, this work will *never* achieve the respect and status it deserves. But if teaching and service are viewed as aspects — dimensions — of scholarship, then they become part of the ongoing concerns of these scholarly communities.

In the academic cathedrals we envision, the members of each scholarly community would, first of all, develop graduate programs that reflected this inclusive view. The chemistry department would view the training of TAs not as someone else's responsibility but as *its* responsibility. The Ph.D. would certify and "mean" that someone was capable not only of specialized research but of representing one's field to students and the larger public as well.

Throughout a scholar's professional life, each field and discipline would reinforce this larger, inclusive conception of scholarship. Annual conventions and association journals would feature and deliberate not only the methods and findings of research but issues of integration, synthesis, and representation — such as the quality of textbooks, the quality of teaching, and the nature of professional service. Thus, scholars who, at some stage of their lives, choose to reflect on their scholarly acts of teaching and service would have respected forums for doing so.

Yet it is one thing to imagine such communities, quite another to restore the present disciplines to such a state. Here, we believe, is where the exciting research now going on about the true nature of teaching and service come in. Lee Shulman's research tells us that in exemplary teaching, knowledge is not just being "transmitted"; it is being "transformed." Great teachers find analogies and metaphors that "transform" concepts into terms that students can understand. Donald Schön, author of *The Reflective Practitioner*, has concluded similar things from his studies of professional practice. Exemplary professionals don't simply "apply" knowledge to a problem; they interact with the situation and develop "theories in action" that guide their work.

Finally, we note that in almost every field and discipline, a growing cadre of scholars is challenging the "positivistic" or "objectivistic" assumptions of the reigning paradigm in their field. These debates — carried on under the banner of "postmodernism" and "quantitative versus qualitative" methods — are about the appropriate content and methods of research. But as they take each field in the direction of more open and inclusive definitions of research, these debates also pave the way for more holistic views of the interrelationships between teaching, research, and service.

There is, in all these matters, a solid basis for optimism. The intellectual groundwork for a more inclusive and holistic conception of scholarship has already been laid. Now we need to articulate that view more clearly, encourage broader discussion and understanding of it, and move toward ways to act out the evolving vision.

Where this logic leads, in our view, is to the need for *peer review* to cover *all aspects* of scholarly life — not only research but teaching and service as well. If teaching and service are aspects of scholarship, then surely the community of scholars has a stake in monitoring how well this scholarship is being performed. Or, to put the matter more bluntly: When and if the scholarly communities apply peer review to teaching and service as they now do to research, then, and only then, will they have finally said, "We *respect* not only research but teaching and service as well."

We hope that those of you who work on portfolios will keep some such vision as this in mind. It follows that the concept of a "teaching portfolio" is itself only one of the tools you'll need. You might prefer to design a "service portfolio," or even a "scholar's portfolio" that embraces the full range of scholarly life. Whatever its size or purpose, if you use it to build a *culture* of professionalism — professionalism in teaching, professionalism in research, and professionalism in service — you will be part of a noble undertaking.

Resources

Bird, Tom. (1989). "The Schoolteacher's Portfolio: An Essay on Possibilities." In *Handbook of Teacher Evaluation: Elementary and Secondary Personnel.* 2nd ed. Edited by J. Millman and L. Darling-Hammond, pp. 241-255. Newbury Park, Calif.: Sage.

Boyer, Ernest L. (1990). *Scholarship Reconsidered: Priorities of the Professoriate.* Princeton, N.J.: Carnegie Foundation for the Advancement of Teaching.

Collins, Angelo. (1991). "Portfolios for Biology Teacher Assessment." *Journal of School Personnel Evaluation in Education* 5(2):147-167.

Edgerton, Russell. (1991). *The Teaching Portfolio as a Display of Best Work.* Paper presented at the National Conference on Higher Education, American Association for Higher Education, Washington, D.C.

Fayne, H. (1991). *Practicing What We Preach: Key Issues in Faculty Evaluation.* Paper presented at the annual meeting of the American Association of Colleges for Teacher Education, Atlanta, Ga.

Foster, S.F., T. Harrap, and G.C. Page. (1983). "The Teaching Dossier." *Higher Education in Europe* 8(2):45-53.

Hutchings, P.A. (1991). "The Teaching Portfolio." *The Department Chair* 2(1):33-35.

King, B. (1990). *Linking Portfolios With Standardized Exercises: One Example From the Teacher Assessment Project.* (Technical Report). Stanford, Calif.: Stanford University, School of Education, Teacher Assessment Project.

Millis, Barbara J. (1991). "Putting the Teaching Portfolio in Context." *To Improve the Academy* 10:215-232.

Schön, Donald. (1983). *The Reflective Practitioner.* New York: Basic Books.

Seldin, Peter. (1991). *The Teaching Portfolio: A Practical Guide to Improved Performance and Promotion/Tenure Decisions.* Bolton, Mass.: Anker Publishing.

———, and L. Annis. (1990). "The Teaching Portfolio." *Journal of Staff, Program, and Organization Development* 8(4):197-201.

Shore, B.M., et al. (1986). *The Teaching Dossier: A Guide to Its Preparation and Use.* Rev. ed. Montreal: Canadian Association of University Teachers.

Shulman, Lee. (In press). *Toward a Pedagogy of Cases: Case Methods in Teacher Education.* Edited by Judith Shulman. New York: Teachers College Press.

_____. (1989). "Toward a Pedagogy of Substance." *AAHE Bulletin* 41(10):8-13.

_____. (1988). "A Union of Insufficiencies: Strategies for Teacher Assessment in a Period of Education Reform." *Educational Leadership* 46(3):36-41.

Stark, Joan S., and W. McKeachie. (1991). *National Center for Research to Improve Postsecondary Teaching and Learning: Final Report.* Ann Arbor, Mich.: NCRIPTAL.

Vavrus, L., and R. Calfee. (1988). *A Research Strategy for Assessing Teachers of Elementary Literacy: The Promise of Performance Portfolios.* Paper presented at the annual meeting of the National Reading Conference, Tucson.

Vavrus, L., and A. Collins. (1991). "Portfolio Documentation and Assessment Center Exercises: A Marriage Made for Teacher Assessment." *Teacher Education Quarterly* 18(3):13-39.

Wolf, Kenneth. (1991). "The Schoolteacher's Portfolio: Practical Issues in Design, Implementation, and Evaluation." *Phi Delta Kappan* October, pp. 129-136.

Campus Practice

A number of campuses are now using the teaching portfolio. What follows here are summaries of practice (much of it in quite early stages) on a variety of campuses. The list is not meant to be exhaustive; nor is it meant to model "best" practice. Our intent, rather, is to represent a range of practices and institutional types, along with information about contacting each campus.

Update: For more detailed descriptions of portfolio use on campus, see AAHE's 1993 publication profiling twenty-five campuses.

* * * * *

Ball State University

More than 100 faculty members have volunteered to participate in a project to develop teaching portfolios that was led by consultant Peter Seldin, professor of management at Pace University. AAHE provided initial seed money to launch the project, which was completed with university funds. The portfolios contain statements of teaching responsibilities, personal reflective statements, syllabi, summaries of student course ratings, and other elective items. Faculty have used the portfolios to improve teaching and to document effectiveness when seeking new positions or being reviewed for promotion and tenure.

> *Contacts:* Judith Roepke, Associate Provost; Tony Edmonds, Chair, History; Mark Fissell, Director, Center for Teaching and Learning; Leo Hodlofski, Assistant Professor, Foreign Languages; Pam Reigle, Instructor, Management Science; Ray Schackelford, Professor, Industry and Technology
> Ball State University
> Muncie, IN 47306

University of Colorado at Boulder

The University of Colorado at Boulder's Faculty Teaching Excellence Program and the Department of Communications are collaborating on a pilot project during the 1991-92 school year to test the use of teaching portfolios. Faculty and teaching assistants who wish to document their teaching for promotion or tenure review or for a job search will be assisted in the development and assembly of their portfolios; an additional and equally important purpose is the improvement of teaching. The project has received the endorsement of the chancellor and the vice chancellor of academic affairs. Depending on the success of this preliminary venture, the program might be expanded to other departments at the university.

> *Contact:* Mary Ann Shea, Director
> Faculty Teaching Excellence Program
> Campus Box 360
> University of Colorado at Boulder
> Boulder, CO 80309

Dalhousie University

Dalhousie has adopted a statement on the teaching dossier that specifies that faculty members are expected to document their teaching effectiveness by collecting and presenting relevant materials. The Office of Instructional Development and Technology offers assistance to faculty in the development of their portfolios. The office is preparing a guide illustrating items for inclusion and has presented a professional-development workshop on performance evaluation and the teaching dossier. The portfolio is designed to be used by promotion and tenure review committees and is also expected to improve teaching performance by encouraging faculty to reflect on their teaching activities.

Contact: W. Alan Wright, Executive Director
Office of Instructional Development and Technology
Dalhousie University
Halifax, Nova Scotia, B3H 3J5 Canada

The Evergreen State College

Portfolios constitute the key component in faculty evaluation at Evergreen; they are part of a unique contract system through which faculty are reviewed for reappointment. All faculty maintain an updated portfolio documenting their performance in the areas of teaching, meeting committments, planning curriculum, and participating in college affairs. Portfolios include self-, student, peer, and other evaluations; descriptions of syllabi, programs, and activities; evaluations of student work; and other materials the faculty member chooses to include.

Contact: Priscilla Bowerman
Academic Dean and Faculty Member
The Evergreen State College
Olympia, WA 98505

Gordon College

At each three-year review, faculty at Gordon submit artifacts of and reflections on their teaching. They are expanding the notion of portfolios to be used as a part of their active faculty-development plan. In summer 1991, a group of senior faculty (one from each of the five divisions of the college) will be developing portfolios that will be the centerpiece of discussion at faculty-development workshops. The hope is that teaching portfolios can then become the vehicle for increased mentoring of junior faculty and an opportunity for more and better dialogue about teaching and learning.

Contact: Jonathan Raymond
Dean of the Faculty
Gordon College
Wenham, MA 01984

University of Maryland University College

Faculty who have been nominated for Excellence in Teaching Awards assemble extensive portfolios containing such items as student ratings, course syllabi, classroom observation reports, recommendations, and personal statements of teaching philosophy. A five-member student/faculty committee reviews the portfolios. The Office of Faculty Development plans to expand the use of portfolios by running workshops and assisting a pilot group of faculty volunteers to assemble and maintain dossiers. In addition, University College plans to extend its present Peer Visitation Program by training participants in that program to serve as faculty consultants to assist their colleagues in preparing teaching portfolios.

> *Contact:* Barbara Millis, Assistant Dean
> Office of Faculty Development
> University of Maryland University College
> University Boulevard at Adelphi Road
> College Park, MD 20742-1660

Miami-Dade Community College

As part of a larger teaching and learning project at Miami-Dade, the college has adopted official policy and procedures regarding the use of teaching portfolios in promotion and tenure considerations and in the judging for the award of Endowed Teaching Chairs. The 1991-92 year will be the first year in which the practice will be implemented. Based on the work of a Teaching Excellence committee, which developed a set of twenty-nine criteria of good teaching, standards for teaching effectiveness have been set across the college, though some departments might have additional requirements. The teaching portfolios may contain reviews from the chair and peers, student works with teacher comments, videotapes, and a standard self-assessment form. The college is providing training in the assembly and evaluation of portfolios, as well as in classroom observation.

> *Contact:* Mardee Jenrette, Director
> Teaching/Learning Project
> Miami-Dade Community College
> 300 N.E. Second Ave.
> Miami, FL 33132

University of Nebraska at Lincoln

Several units at the University of Nebraska at Lincoln — including English, psychology, and the College of Agriculture — are using teaching portfolios in their evaluation plans. Participants in this work note that the culture of each department is different and that each devises its own unique set of standards and formats. Portfolios were introduced as part of a project supported by the Fund for the Improvement of Postsecondary Education on rewarding teaching at research universities. Now in its third year, the project has involved almost thirty departments in a variety of colleges.

> *Contact:* Leverne Barrett, Associate Professor, Agriculture Education
> Daniel Bernstein, Professor, Psychology
> Robert Narveson, Professor, English
> University of Nebraska
> Lincoln, NE 68588-0333

New Community College of Baltimore

The New Community College of Baltimore has been using portfolios for two years, both to improve teaching and for decision making related to contract renewal; it requires a self-report portfolio as part of the evaluation process. The portfolio contains documentation of accomplishments in four main categories: (1) teaching effectiveness (further divided into motivation skills, interpersonal skills, and intellectual skills); (2) special contributions to the college and community; (3) credentials and professional development; and (4) professional associations and awards. These categories are rated by the dean and peers.

> *Contact:* Raymond Yannuzzi
> Acting Vice President for Academic Affairs
> New Community College of Baltimore
> 2901 Liberty Heights Ave.
> Baltimore, MD 21215-7893

Otterbein College

All faculty at Otterbein submit a teaching dossier in years when renewal, tenure, and promotion decisions are made and prepare a briefer report for annual review. The Education Department has expanded that evaluation plan and requires its faculty to complete a full portfolio assessment each year, which consists of plans for the year, descriptions of types of support needed, documentation of accomplishments, and narrative reflections. The college notes, in particular, that the portfolio increases dialogue among faculty about course content and teaching methods, making it a vehicle for department development, as well as an individual faculty development tool.

> *Contact:* Harriet R. Fayne, Chair, Education Department
> Ralph Pearson, Vice President for Academic Affairs
> Otterbein College
> Westerville, OH 43081

University of Pittsburgh

The Office of Faculty Development administers the judging for Distinguished Teaching Awards. All nominees must submit a teaching portfolio that supplies documentation in five categories and meets specific guidelines adapted from Peter Seldin's work; *Sourcebook for Evaluation of Teaching*, by Barbara Gross Davis; and *The Teaching Dossier*, by the Canadian Association of University Teachers. A number of departments are currently discussing the use of teaching portfolios on a more extended basis. Portfolio guidelines and additional information are available upon request.

> *Contact:* Margaret Waterman, Director
> Office of Faculty Development
> 1701 Cathedral of Learning
> University of Pittsburgh
> Pittsburgh, PA 15260

Syracuse University

The Center for Instructional Development offers to work with any instructors who would like to assemble a teaching portfolio. Typically these are second-year faculty who are preparing for their third-year review and TAs who are involved in job searches. The institution advocates that a portfolio contain (1) information about the context of the teaching, such as past and present teaching responsibilities and accomplishments; (2) a statement of current goals; (3) an action plan to be worked out with the chair; and (4) the presentation of current evidence relative to teaching goals. The Center gives presentations to deans and department chairs outlining those recommendations for putting together and evaluating portfolios, but departments independently determine guidelines for use of portfolios in the review process. The engineering school has formal requirements for the use of portfolios, as does the Newhouse School of Public Communications.

> *Contact:* Peter J. Gray
> Director of Evaluation and Research
> Center for Instructional Development
> Syracuse University
> 111 Waverly Avenue, Suite 220
> Syracuse, NY 13244-2320

Portfolios at the K-12 level

A number of practitioners, researchers, and organizations are exploring the use of teaching portfolios at the K-12 level. Teacher-education programs are asking preservice teachers to construct teaching portfolios as a way to stimulate teacher reflection; school districts are using teaching portfolios as part of their teacher-evaluation process; the National Board for Professional Teaching Standards (drawing on work from Stanford's Teacher Assessment Project reported on in this monograph) is exploring the use of teaching portfolios in developing a voluntary, national certification system.

A *clearinghouse* on teaching portfolios used in the above settings has now been established. Initially, the clearinghouse will collect materials, develop an annotated bibliography, and establish a directory of individuals and organizations working with teaching portfolios.

> *Contact:* Kenneth Wolf
> Far West Laboratory
> 730 Harrison Street
> San Francisco, CA 94107

For Product Safety Concerns and Information please contact our EU
representative GPSR@taylorandfrancis.com Taylor & Francis Verlag GmbH,
Kaufingerstraße 24, 80331 München, Germany

Printed and bound by CPI Group (UK) Ltd, Croydon, CR0 4YY

11/04/2025

01844013-0001